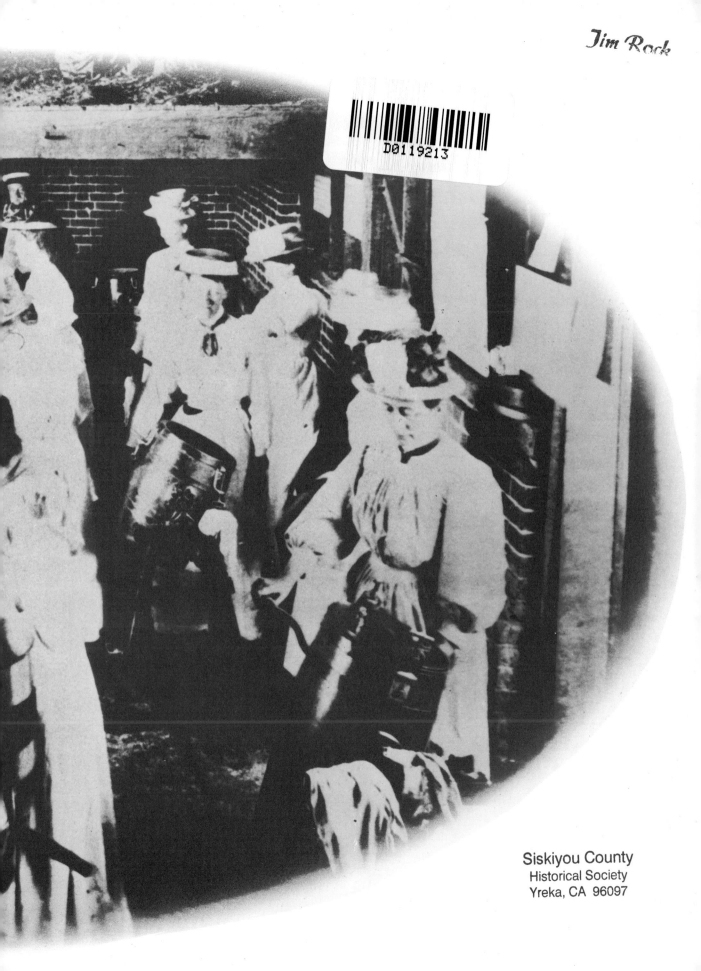

Jim Rock

Kitchen Antiques

Mary Norwak

Kitchen Antiques

PRAEGER PUBLISHERS New York

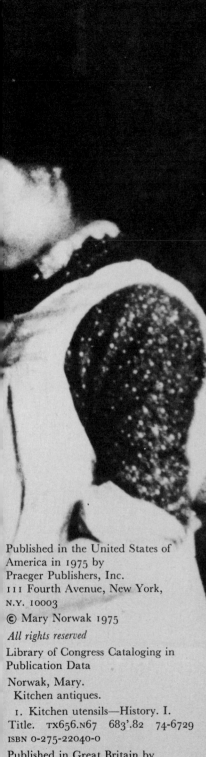

Contents

Published in the United States of
America in 1975 by
Praeger Publishers, Inc.
111 Fourth Avenue, New York,
N.Y. 10003
© Mary Norwak 1975
All rights reserved
Library of Congress Cataloging in
Publication Data
Norwak, Mary.
  Kitchen antiques.
  1. Kitchen utensils—History. I.
Title. TX656.N67 683'.82 74-6729
ISBN 0-275-22040-0
Published in Great Britain by
Ward Lock Limited, London
Printed in Great Britain

Introduction 7

The Fireplace and Cooking Equipment 11

Kitchen Furniture 27

The Dairy 39

The Laundry 53

Cleaning the House 67

Storage and Preservation 73

Moulds, Cutters and Serving Equipment 84

Labour-Saving Devices 95

Convenience Foods and Cleaning Materials 109

Billheads, Account Books and Manuscript Recipes 122

Kitchens, Houses and Museums to Visit 131

Sources of Illustrations 132

Index 133

Acknowledgments

This book could not have been written without the kindness and generosity of many people who shared their knowledge. My particular thanks are due to The Sulgrave Manor Board; Lord and Lady Braye; Bruce Tattersall of The Wedgwood Museum; Pauline Millward of Halifax Museums and Art Galleries Service; Alison Heath, Schools Advisor at The Geffrye Museum; Christopher Sykes of Woburn; Evelyn Vigeon of City of Salford Art Galleries and Museums; Constance Purser of The Stedman Homestead, Aston Munslow; The Marquis of Bath; R. J. Butcher of Colman's, Norwich; John Ruffle of City of Birmingham Museums and Art Gallery; Pamela Murray of the Museum of Staffordshire Life; Enid Porter of The County Folk Museum, Cambridge.

I am also greatly indebted to Sue Unstead, a patient editor who undertook valuable picture research; Rosemary Klein for her American research into both text and pictures; and Christine Tewson who made the manuscript readable.

Introduction

Kitchenware is timeless and international. Pestles and mortars were used in Babylon in 2500 BC, colanders and frying pans have been found in the ruins of Pompeii, and pastry cutters were part of the kitchen equipment of France in AD 200. An Elizabethan entering a modern kitchen might be confused by electrical gadgets, but would be perfectly at home with ladles and moulds, rolling pins and saucepans, kettles and spice jars, the materials and designs of which have scarcely changed in hundreds of years. Likewise a Scandinavian housewife could work in an Italian kitchen, an American in an Australian one, and women from all these countries could produce a fair meal in an eighteenth-century farmhouse setting.

The reason is a simple one. Family life started round the fire and centred on the cooking which took place there. Houses were built around the kitchen, which also served as a living room and often as a bedroom. Simple furniture and equipment for this room was made to suit the housewife's needs and comfort. Before the introduction of the kitchen range in the early nineteenth century, all cooking was done over an open fire, which was originally set in the centre of the room, then from the twelfth century at the side. Pots, pans and baking sheets were suspended over the flames, and their design and shape changed little for well over two thousand years.

Kitchen bygones are in the main simple, straightforward and utilitarian, well-used and well-worn. They are strong and practical, of sturdy construction and of great functional beauty. They are not made of precious materials; their craftsmanship is not exquisite; they rarely carry a maker's name, nor the blessing of any expert. But to people who care for simple beauty, they are of great value.

Many items were made by local craftsmen. The blacksmith made cooking forks and pot hooks, dippers and strainers, toasters and trivets and any items constructed in wrought iron. Saucepans, pots and kettles were the work of the coppersmith, or cast-iron foundry jobs. Tinsmiths made many small cooking utensils, while peddlers supplied tinware and brushes, which they carried in packs on their backs, or on horseback.

Many everyday household items were made at home, particularly in America, where the self-supporting settlers were prepared to make their own brooms, brushes, doormats, bread troughs, cheese hoops,

7

butter paddles and washboards. Some items were sold in general or hardware stores, but in the nineteenth century manufacturing firms employed salesmen to introduce their wares at bazaars, tea meetings and the like. Mail order became popular in the late nineteenth and early twentieth century, and general stores issued catalogues offering food, clothing and hardware.

Kitchen antiques are above all a vital key to the social history of the past thousand years. Through them we can trace economic developments, the changing face of fashion, the influence of town on country and vice versa, and the interchange of ideas between countries and continents. Collectors of kitchenware find that they do not become involved only with single categories or specific materials, but with the whole range of kitchen equipment, studying the ways in which it was used and the setting in which it originally appeared.

The quantity of kitchenware available to the collector is almost overwhelming. I have tried to select key items to indicate a whole range of antiques or bygones which can be collected, but many of these are fast disappearing. Luckily, many museums have been aware of the value of simple domestic items, but every day interesting pieces are thrown out by housewives in favour of modern machines, and those items which do survive are often difficult to identify or value. They can frequently be found at sales or on junk stalls, or in use in cottages and farmhouses, and are only recently being rescued and promoted to genuine antique shops, for they do not always qualify as antiques on the basis of age or material value.

It is difficult to assess the value of these items in the homes of their original owners. Many people in the eighteenth century, and earlier, owned little but their kitchen furnishings and equipment and some bedding. An English auction record of 1773 gives some interesting prices. A long tin fish kettle was 2s., and a round one 1s. 6d. A 'cullender, cake pan, cheese toaster, a plate cover and patty pans' 2s., and 5 red earthen pots 1s. Four ash chairs fetched 10s., and 10 knives and forks in a box 4s. Four brushes, a dustpan and a toastfork were worth 2s. 6d., the same price as one pair of Delft dishes and 3 plates. Everyday kitchen items were expensive in comparison with the cost of glass, china and furniture, which today fetch high prices in the saleroom (mahogany claw table 10s.; a corner cupboard 5s.; 6 wine glasses with worm stems 2s.).

Curiously enough, nearly a century later in 1854, kitchen and dairy items still fetched comparatively high prices in spite of increasing production. From a later record, a set of shoe brushes cost 3s., 2 tin funnels, strainer and warmer 2s., and a tin tea kettle the same price, while a spice cupboard fetched 1s., a pair of Wedgwood jugs 3s. 6d., and a complete 12-person tea and breakfast service £1.

In Colonial America basic equipment was even more highly prized. An inventory of the estate of Lieut. John Buttolph of Wethersfield in 1692 listed a mortar and pestle 6s., 'ye great brass kettle' £4.18s., 3 skillets 15*s*. and 2 iron pots and pot hooks 42*s*. A valuation of the estate of prosperous Solomon Fussell of Philadelphia in 1762 showed less concern for the necessities of life:

1 Large Brass Kettle or Pan 10*s*.; 1 Morter & Pessel & 1 Sauspan 2*s*. 6d.; and 3 Salts, 3 Mustard Potts, 1 Can, 13 Pastipans, 1 Cullender, a Pepper Box, a Coffee Mill and Tea Kettle all Old 7*s*. 6*d*.

The time scale of this book extends to 1914, when the domestic scene suffered an upheaval from which it has never recovered. Kitchen staff disappeared from most houses, family life changed beyond recognition, modern inventions revolutionized housework, and the old methods of work and necessary equipment were discarded. Perhaps the kitchen has become a cleaner and more functional place to work in, but its simple beauty has gone for ever.

1 The Fireplace and Cooking Equipment

Although in large houses the kitchen was often built as a separate unit situated away from the main house, in most homes the kitchen was the most important, and indeed often the only room. It was certainly the only room with a fire and naturally was the place where the family lived during the day, and often slept at night. Early American settlers began their houses by building the kitchen, fire-room, or common-room, which remained the one living area until greater prosperity allowed additional parts of the house to be built.

In the earliest permanent houses the fire was situated in the centre of the room with smoke escaping through a central chimney. The disadvantages of this were obvious, and fires were moved to wall hearths. This type of fireplace, known as a down hearth, consisted of a slab of stone or iron raised slightly above floor level on which the fire was made. At first all cooking was done in or over the fire, but later, in larger houses, ovens for baking were built into the chimney itself. The earliest ovens were built at the back of the fire, directly over it, or slightly to one side. The basic oven had a round floor and a dome-shaped top like a beehive to keep in the heat. The opening was an arch with a sill, and a simple door was made from a flat board placed across the entrance. Tin doors later replaced wooden ones, until cast iron became popular. The iron doors were swung on hinges, but the inner door of wood or tin was often retained to keep the oven airtight.

The kitchen at Sulgrave Manor, the ancestral Oxfordshire home of the Washington family, provides a fine example of a large fireplace and the way in which the cooking was done. The original kitchen equipment was dispersed, but a complete kitchen was later purchased from a manor house at Weston Corbett in Hampshire so that the Sulgrave kitchen could be restored exactly as it was when Laurence Washington built the house in 1560.

The kitchen is nearly 17 feet long, with its ceiling supported by a single massive oak beam. The great square chimney opening is 10 feet wide and nearly 4 feet deep, with an oak chimney-beam 5 feet from the ground. Along the front of this hangs a short frill of material to act as a draught 'sharpener'. Fixed to the chimney beam and extending beyond it is a long moulded mantleshelf to hold kitchen utensils. The fireplace hearth itself is 10 inches high; this helped to secure a better draught, and made a more convenient height for cooking.

The open hearth fire at Strangers' Hall, Norwich. At the back of the fireplace is an adjustable chimney crane, which could be swung out over the fireplace. The cauldron is suspended on a wrought-iron ratchet-hanger, and in front of the hearth, supported by two firedogs, is a simple pronged spit, which was turned by the clockwork jack above the fireplace. The smoke jack to the right was driven by paddle wheels in the chimney which were turned by the upward rush of hot air from the fire.

Inside the chimney corner on the left is a semi-circular niche, the lower part filled in and forming a charcoal brazier with a wrought-iron top for the heating of flatirons, and below it is a wrought-iron oven door. On the right of the chimney opening is the ancient bread oven, which extends far into the wall beneath the kitchen stairs. Its arched, tunnel-like roof has rounded sides, and the whole is lined with fireproof brick. It is 3 feet deep, 2 feet 10 inches wide, and 18 inches high, with a wrought-iron door with a long-handled latch. In front of it is a ledge, on which to rest the peel or bread-shovel when drawing out the loaves.

Sticks from the hedgerow tied into bundles served as fuel, and were set alight in the oven. When burnt through, the ashes were raked out with an iron peel and the oven was mopped out with damp rags. The surrounding brick was still hot enough to bake the loaves, known as batch-cakes, which were placed in the oven with a wooden peel. This oven was also used for meat dishes, pies and tarts, which were placed on thin iron plates or baking sheets, and set in the oven with the wooden peel. The iron peel was used for removing the heavy baking sheets and earthenware dishes when cooking was completed.

In the Sulgrave kitchen there is also a hearth-oven occupying the centre of the raised hearth. It is lined with iron and has a wrought-iron door fitted with long strap-hinges and a small, circular, adjustable vent-hole in the centre. It is supported upon either side by the hearth-bricks, and the fire was constructed on top of it. The oven is covered by a strong iron slab forming a hotplate, measuring nearly 4 feet long and 3 feet wide, extending to the back of the hearth. The oven could also be heated from below by means of hot ashes placed in a narrow brick-lined channel extending from the front of the hearth under the level of the floor to the back of the oven, and opening to the back at the base of the chimney. Its entrance is covered by a small iron trapdoor, set flush into the stone floor of the kitchen. This oven was very hot, and was used chiefly for cooking pastry, as well as for warming plates or keeping food hot.

Such an elaborate fireplace was, of course, only found in manor houses and farmhouses, and many cottages managed without an oven at all, or with only one. In the eighteenth century some fireplaces had two ovens, one placed on top of the other. The lower oven was often only roughly built, and was used for preparing ashes for making a washing solution known as lye, which is more fully described in Chapter 4. As coal was used increasingly as a fuel for cooking in the nineteenth century, fireplaces became smaller, and the domed round oven was replaced by an oblong-shaped bake oven with an arched top.

The use of the open fire over so many centuries necessitated an enormous range of equipment and implements for cooking, and for tending the fire. It was not always easy to start a fire freshly each morning, but it was also dangerous to leave a fire uncovered at night, for fire could destroy not only the original house, but often a whole street or village. A curfew or couvre-feu was used to keep a small fire

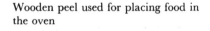

Wooden peel used for placing food in the oven

Opposite A fireplace at the Castle Museum, York, shows the way in which open fireplaces were gradually adapted to built-in ovens and ranges. The oven to the left has been built in over its own fire-box, while a portion of the fireplace remains open, and is fitted with a simple chimney crane for suspending kettles and pans.

warm and ready for rapid rekindling the next morning. The early iron curfew or 'nightcap' was shaped like a bell cut in half, with a small loop handle to lift it. Sometimes these were made in brass, and those with a hook could be attached to the fire-grate in living rooms. Another form of the fire cover is cylindrical in shape, tapering slightly at the top, and with a long handle. Not only was this used to cover the fire, but it was sometimes inverted to hold a few embers for a small side fire, or to heat a bedroom.

Cooking pots had to be suspended over the open fires for boiling. Originally the pots were hung on hooks from a wooden lug pole resting on ledges or 'lugs' high up on the sides of the chimney. However, these poles charred easily, and by the seventeenth century a wrought-iron chimney crane or reckon was in use. The American settlers continued to use lug poles until the introduction of the crane in 1720. The earliest type of crane consisted of a horizontal bar forged to an iron hinge which was attached to the back of the hearth. The bar could be swung backwards and forwards over the fire to the required position. In later and more elaborate examples the height of the cranes could be adjusted by raising a lever, which was held in position by circular studs. These cranes were usually made by the local blacksmith and could be extremely ornamental.

Where there was no adjustable crane, the pot was suspended above the fire from a pot-hook, an S-shaped iron hook. Three- or four-piece hooks with racks and loops were called cotrails, jibcrooks or tramelles, and these could be adjusted to raise or lower the pot. The American trammel, known in England as a ratchet-hanger, was a more elaborate height-adjuster. This was an iron bar curved at the top with a flat iron attachment looking like a coarse saw. The curved end of the ratchet was hooked over the lug pole; at the lower end a loop and hook was

Wrought-iron double trammel, which could be adjusted by the notches on the hangers; Pennsylvania Dutch, 18th century

A basket spit supported by firedogs. On the left is the wheel which was fitted with a pulley mechanism to turn the spit.

14

Above Wrought-iron ratchet-hanger for suspending pots over an open hearth; English, 18th century

Right Tin roasting or reflector oven used in New England about 1790. The food was spitted so that it could be turned and cooked evenly.

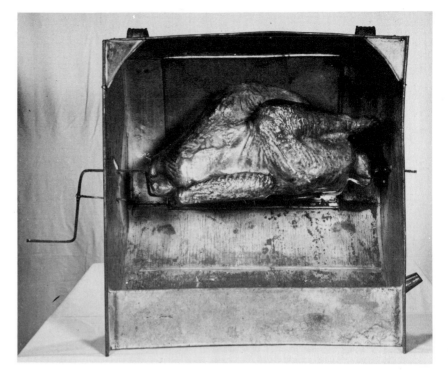

attached to one of the teeth of the ratchet. A double trammel was sometimes used to hold two pots.

Meat was roasted in front of the fire on a spit suspended over a dripping-pan. The most simple type was an iron stick supported on either side by firedogs or andirons. The spit was rotated by turning a handle. More elaborate examples were fitted with a pulley mechanism and the handle was turned by the cook-boy or turnspit. In some cases the spit was fitted with a wheel, which was driven round by a small dog placed in a wooden cage or drum. Large joints were roasted on a spit fitted with prongs, which held the meat firmly and could be adjusted. Fish or poultry were cooked in a basket or cradle spit. This was a cage-like arrangement made up of steel bars, which could be removed to insert the food.

In the eighteenth century some spits were connected by a rope to the wheel of an elaborate weighted jack. When wound up, the jack slowly rotated the spit before the fire. Another variant was the smoke jack, in which a paddle wheel in the chimney was driven round by the hot air rising from the fire. A nineteenth-century invention for roasting meat was the clockwork bottle jack made of brass or japanned metal, and hung from a bracket fitted to the mantleshelf. The cylindrical jack contained an internal clockwork mechanism, and the small joints suspended from a hook below the jack rotated over a dripping pan.

The bottle jack could also be used in front of a domed iron or tinplate reflector oven, which speeded up the rate of cooking by reflecting the heat of the fire, as well as acting as a shield for the cook. This type of reflector was also sometimes fitted with shelves so that it could be used for baking food. Apple and rabbit roasters were a popular American adaptation of the reflector oven.

This type of fire shield is often erroneously known as a Dutch oven. In fact, the Dutch oven was a three-legged iron pot with a loop handle and a closely-fitting lid. This 'oven' could be placed in the fire, and hot peat or ashes heaped on the lid so that even bread could be baked inside. This type of cooker was known in Ireland as a bastable, and was in use until recent times.

Below right Cast-iron Dutch oven used for cooking in an open hearth; American, late 18th century. Hot ashes were heaped on the lid, and the oven would reach a high enough temperature for baking bread.

Below Bronze skillet; English, 18th century. The handle is cast with the name Wasbrough.

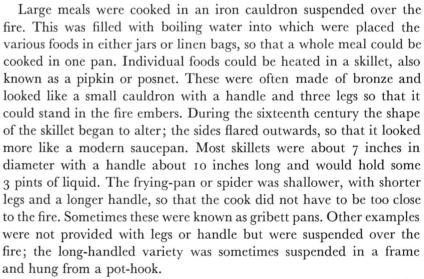

Large meals were cooked in an iron cauldron suspended over the fire. This was filled with boiling water into which were placed the various foods in either jars or linen bags, so that a whole meal could be cooked in one pan. Individual foods could be heated in a skillet, also known as a pipkin or posnet. These were often made of bronze and looked like a small cauldron with a handle and three legs so that it could stand in the fire embers. During the sixteenth century the shape of the skillet began to alter; the sides flared outwards, so that it looked more like a modern saucepan. Most skillets were about 7 inches in diameter with a handle about 10 inches long and would hold some 3 pints of liquid. The frying-pan or spider was shallower, with shorter legs and a longer handle, so that the cook did not have to be too close to the fire. Sometimes these were known as gribett pans. Other examples were not provided with legs or handle but were suspended over the fire; the long-handled variety was sometimes suspended in a frame and hung from a pot-hook.

As ranges and cookers with hotplates came into use, the need for legged utensils diminished. Early pans were very heavy, made of cast iron, with long handles. Larger houses often had a number of pans for special purposes, usually made in copper, with side lugs instead of handles. Ham kettles were large, lidded pans, fish kettles were narrower ones, and preserving pans or cheese pans for heating milk were shallower and round without lids. Small copper pans with lids and long handles

Copper saucepans and frying pan; English, mid-19th century. Pans of similar shapes were also made in heavy iron.

were used in sets in a shallow tray or *bain-marie* of hot water to cook food gently, or keep it warm.

When the housewife wished to pour water from a kettle without lifting it up or burning her hands, she used a kettle-tilter. The kettle was suspended over the fire by an arrangement of hooks, and an adjustable handle allowed her to tip up the kettle. This was also known as a lazy-back or idle-back.

A similar kind of gadget was called a hastener. This was an iron bar, about 19 inches long, with a lip at either end so that it could be fitted over the bars of the grate. Attached to this bar was a heavy iron ring, on which the cooking pot was placed. The ring was divided into two halves and hinged across the middle; one half could be raised by means of a prop, thus tilting the pot towards the fire to speed up the cooking.

Above Two bread toasters; American, late 18th century. The racks could be revolved so that the bread was toasted on both sides.

Below Wrought-iron rotary broiler; American, 18th century. It is fitted with short legs and was designed to stand in front of the fire. The top could be turned to brown all sides of the food.

Many foods, like toast, cheese or small birds, were cooked in front of the fire on spiked implements. A type of toasting fork used in America was mounted on a small stand. A more elaborate version was the toasting dog, or standing toaster, which incorporated a circular- or triangular-shaped frame of iron with a number of spikes to hold the food. The meat toaster usually had a dripping-pan beneath, while the bread toaster, which looked more like a modern toast rack, had to be revolved so that the bread was toasted on both sides.

A variation on the toaster was the lark spit, a series of hooks on a wire rack with a dripping-pan. The spit stood about 6 inches high, and the little birds could be cooked on both sides without being unhooked.

Small pieces of meat could be grilled directly over the fire with a gridiron, which consisted of a number of iron bars set in a frame, and fitted with a long handle so that the cook did not have to stand too near the fire. The hanging gridiron was designed to be suspended from the bars of the grate; it resembled a flat cage, with a drip-tray underneath to catch the fat.

When cooking pots were taken off the fire they were placed on a pot-stand or trivet. Early examples were simply iron triangles or circles mounted on three legs and sometimes fitted with a short handle. Later models were heavily ornamented, and some had a hook so that they could be attached to the bars of the grate. Some trivets were actually pushed into the fire and the cooking pot was placed on top. Four-legged stands, similar to trivets, were designed to go under dripping-pans, while similar devices, known as footmen, were used to hold kettles or dishes of food in other rooms.

A curious type of plate warmer, known as the cat, had six spokes radiating from the centre—three spokes at the top and three at the bottom—and could be used either way up to hold plates. It was sometimes made in wood, but was of more practical use in iron. There was also a plate warmer which looked very similar to the reflector oven. It was mounted on four legs, with shelves and an iron grid at the back to prevent plates from dropping out. The plate warmer could be carried by a handle at the top.

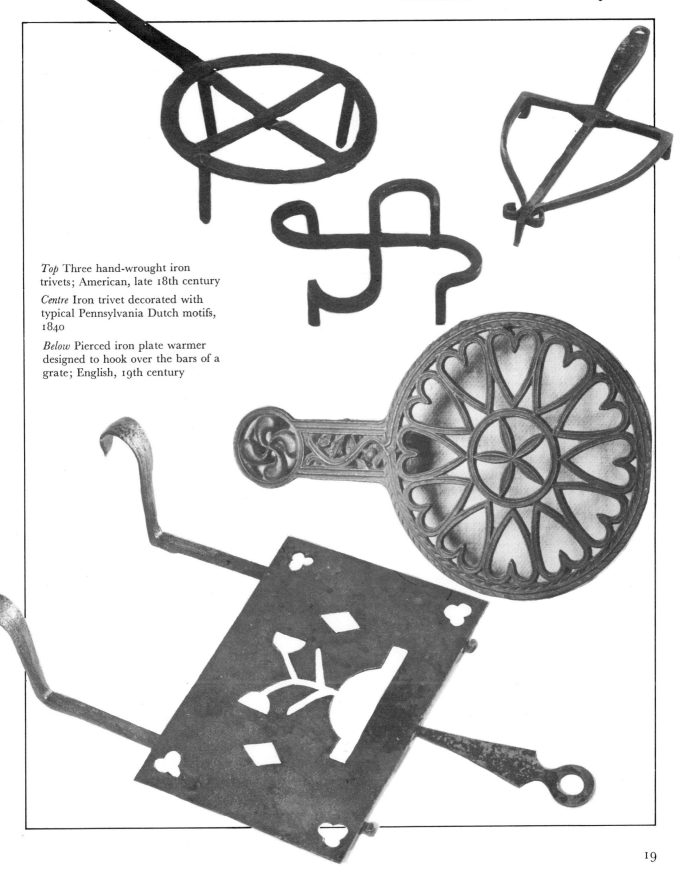

Top Three hand-wrought iron trivets; American, late 18th century

Centre Iron trivet decorated with typical Pennsylvania Dutch motifs, 1840

Below Pierced iron plate warmer designed to hook over the bars of a grate; English, 19th century

Pennsylvania Dutch waffle iron,
early 19th century

The small metal spikes used to dress meat and poultry were stored in a skewer-holder mounted on the wall. This was a rack with small hooks on which the skewers rested. A much larger metal frame fitted with hooks was used to hold meat, and was known as a Dutch crown. The frame was suspended from the ceiling by a ring, and could be raised or lowered as needed. Six or seven hooks were arranged around a circular hoop made of iron or brass. Smoked and preserved meats were hung on these hooks, and sometimes there was also a larger hook in the centre with two prongs, to hold heavier pieces of meat. The Dutch crown might also be hung in the ice house to chill meat.

Bread was not always baked in the oven, but sometimes cooked over the fire. The dough was placed on heavy iron baking sheets, also known as griddles, girdles, brandreths, or branders, with half-hoop handles for suspending them over the open fire. The cooked food was removed with a flat implement known as a baking-iron.

Oatcakes were also cooked over the fire. They were first shaped on a scored riddleboard, then flicked onto a smooth cloth-covered board called a spittle, before being cooked in the fireplace on a hot bakestone, which was made of mudstone, and was polished with a little fat to prevent the oatcake from sticking.

Wafers or waffles have been made from very early times and special wafer irons were used to shape them. These are like long tongs with the jaws made of two flat discs heavily decorated on the inner surface. These irons were originally used to make wafer breads for church services, but they continued in domestic use until the nineteenth century. Batter was poured into the tongs which had been pre-heated and greased; the wafers were then baked over the fire and were removed from the iron with a stick when cooked. The very elaborate irons were used for a light batter; those with a pattern of squares held a thicker batter which produced a more solid biscuit.

A number of long-handled tools were needed in the preparation of food when the cook needed to stay well away from the heat of the fire. Flesh or meat forks were pronged implements on long handles for dealing

Tin skimmers for removing scum and fat, and for lifting food from boiling liquid; American, c. 1900

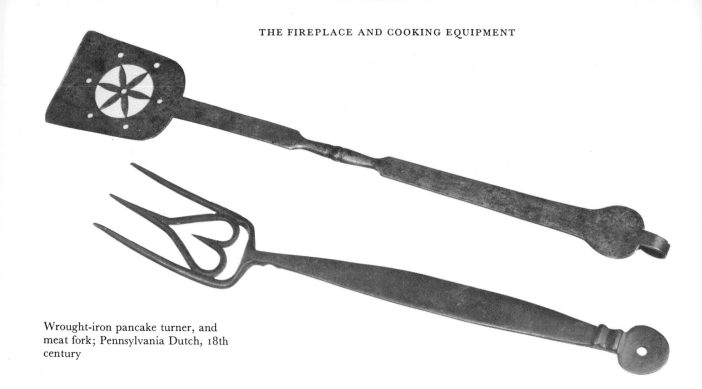

Wrought-iron pancake turner, and meat fork; Pennsylvania Dutch, 18th century

with food on a spit or in an oven. Long-handled flat pierced spoons were used for skimming, while unpierced flat blades on handles were turners for baked goods. Another useful implement was the flip dog or toddy dog, consisting of a long handle with either a tear-shaped or pointed end, which was thrust into the hot embers and then into a drink to heat it and give it a pleasant flavour. The salamander was a long bar of iron with a square or circular iron plate at the end. This was heated in the fire until red-hot and then held over the food to brown it. Some salamanders had short legs on the handle so the implement could be stood over the food; later ones had a hole in the centre of the handle which fitted on to an iron stand.

Although the first iron stove was made in China in the later Han dynasty (AD 25–200), iron cooking stoves did not appear until the end of the eighteenth century. Benjamin Thompson, known as Count Rumford, was a heating engineer, who invented the first cooking range. In 1802 George Bodley, an iron-founder of Exeter, patented a closed-top cooking stove. This had an open fire at the front for roasting, with firebricks on the side of the oven to prevent scorching, and an iron flue leading up the chimney. These were very popular in Devonshire, where the large hotplate was used for scalding milk for cream. The new cookers were bricked into the old open fireplaces and known as kitchen ranges. Portable ranges or kitcheners, with four legs and an iron flue, were American innovations. By the middle of the nineteenth century many old fireplaces were being bricked up and replaced by a cast-iron box with two stove lids on top.

Steam kitchen ranges were patented by one John Slater, a manufacturer of coach springs. Economy and cleanliness were just two of the advantages of his 'patent steamer, roaster, etc.', which he advertised as being built in two parts on either side of a fire. This not only performed all kinds of cooking, but ensured 'a constant supply of Boiling Water for other purposes . . . also the advantage of Warming Baths, with Steam, in Lower & Upper Rooms, Closets & Apartments, at a distance of 100 Feet & upwards, by means of the Kitchen Range Fire'. The cooking could be undertaken 'without causing either too much heat or unpleasant smell'. A smaller version of this stove, known as the Improved Self-Acting Cottage Range was produced by Smith and Welstood in 1880. It is interesting to note in pictures of such ranges that the old methods of cooking still persisted. Pans for boiling food were often suspended over the new stove on the old crane from the original fireplace.

During this same period, gas was first being introduced for cooking, and was later to become popular in towns. The first gas appliance looked like a gridiron perforated with holes, and a pan was placed on this for frying and boiling food. For roasting the grid was set upright so that the gas jets pointed towards meat which was hung in front; a

The 'Improved Self-Acting' cottage range made by Smith & Welstood in 1880 has a side-oven, water heater, small grate and hotplate. This type of range would be fitted into an existing open hearth, and bricked in.

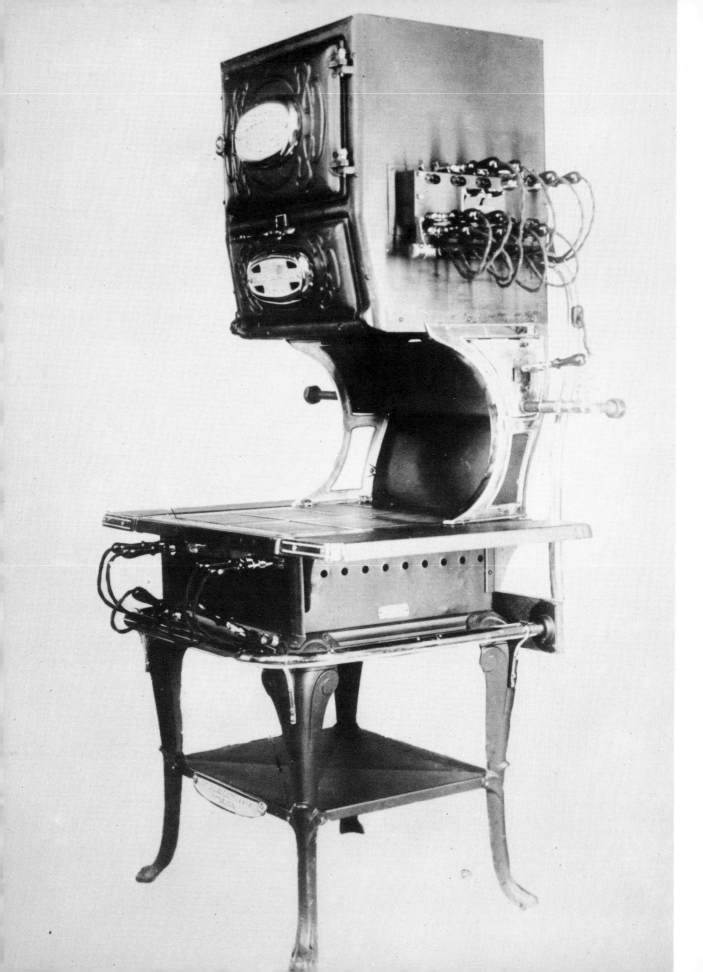

An experimental electric cooker designed by Westinghouse of America in 1908. In later designs the oven was placed beneath the hotplates, but this model has an eye-level oven, a feature of modern cookers.

tin reflector or 'hastener' was placed behind the meat to reflect heat. In 1841 Alexis Soyer introduced gas cookers to the Reform Club in London, but the original cookers were still too cumbersome for home use. Sharp's Gas-Cooking Apparatus, shown at a special exhibition of the Gasfitters' Association, was a vast cylindrical oven on iron claw feet, in which the meat was suspended from a rotating mechanism above the gas burners. The top of the stove contained a large water boiler and had space for two large ham kettles, a stock boiler, and many other saucepans. James Sharp of Northampton, the pioneer of this type of cooking, actually demonstrated cooking fish, fowl, bacon, pudding and greens, which were all prepared in the same steamer, and 'no dish had contracted any unpleasant taste from its neighbour'. Sharp's cooker was subsequently taken up by a number of hotels in the 1830s, but it was not until the second half of the nineteenth century that gas cookers were in use in the home, and housewives could enjoy freedom from the traditional kitchen fire. Oil cookers were in use for a brief period, having the advantage that they were free-standing and did not rely on public supplies of fuel. But these were never really popular, and the electric cooker was the next important development for town kitchens.

The earliest electric cookers were built in cast iron by firms such as Carron. They were solid in construction, but the arrangement of ovens and hotplates differs little from today's designs. An American experimental electric range made by Westinghouse in 1908 was less heavily built, but had an extraordinary collection of plugs on display, and is unusual in that the oven and grill are at eye-level.

2 Kitchen Furniture

It is difficult to imagine how sparsely furnished were kitchens until the middle of the nineteenth century. Those who restore kitchens for display tend to crowd in tables, many chairs, dressers and hanging cupboards loaded down with a display of cooking equipment and tableware. It is as if a housewife had crammed all the furnishings of her dining room and sitting room into the kitchen and then emptied out the contents of every drawer and cupboard.

In reality, early kitchens had little more than a stout table to use for cooking and eating. Perhaps a bench or stools might accompany it, although many poor families ate their meals standing. As an added refinement, there might be a small side table for preparing food. Walls were whitewashed, and there were no mats on the floor because of the danger of fire from an open hearth.

In Colonial America simplicity was essential when furniture had to be imported or home-made, and life was generally hard. Benjamin Franklin, the chandler's son who became a printer, inventor and diplomat, summed it up:

We have an English proverb that says 'He that would thrive must ask his wife'. It was lucky for me that I had one as much dispos'd to industry and frugality as myself. We kept no idle servants, our table was plain and simple, our furniture of the cheapest. One morning being call'd to breakfast, I found it in a china bowl with a spoon of silver! They had been brought for me without my knowledge by my wife. She thought her husband deserv'd a silver spoon and china bowl as well as any of his neighbours. This was the first appearance of plate and china in our house which afterwards in course of years, as our wealth increas'd, augmented gradually to several hundred pounds in value.

This careful frugality was also evident in England, when few could afford conspicuous expenditure. Inventories of households in south-east England in 1638 list little furniture. One refers to 'A tablle, three Stoolles and a Forme and 3 Cheyres' as the sole household furniture, except for a bedstead, belonging to Jenne Barnard, a widow. Richard Bridgman, a weaver, had 'One Table & a frame, 2 Formes, two little ioyne stooles, the bench and bench board, one little playne table', and few households had more than one table and a couple of benches in the whole house. In 1681 prosperous Edward Huttly, owner of 24 pewter dishes and a pewter flagon, left only 1 table in the kitchen, but his hall

Bow-back and comb Windsor chair with rockers; American, 18th century

27

Pennsylvania Dutch dough trough with kneading table top in unstained pine wood, mid-18th century

had 2 tables, 4 forms, 3 chairs and 2 joint stools, indicating that middle-class families were beginning to use a separate room for living and eating, and that the kitchen was considered as a workroom.

In 1708 Henry Mansfeild, a yeoman farmer with a large house and servants, had 'one long table, 1 forme, 6 chairs, 1 joyned stoole' in the kitchen, and even more furniture in the parlour. By 1749 farmer John Portway had a total of 25 chairs and 5 tables in his house.

American inventories show a similar change in prosperity. William Googe, an unsuccessful farmer in Massachusetts, died in 1646 leaving little but a chest, a chair, an old chair and a stool. On his death in 1675, blacksmith Daniel Howard, from the same area, had a two-roomed house, and left 'a little Joyned table, 6 old Chayers', in addition to a variety of chests. Dr Avery in 1691 had 4 chairs and a table in the kitchen, and a year later, John Buttolph, a prosperous farmer and merchant, had 2 tables with 10 chairs and stools. By the eighteenth century Colonial homes were increasing in size like their English counterparts, and while the kitchen retained only a table and perhaps some stools, William Hasey, a yeoman who died in 1754, had 18 chairs and an oval table in his 'best room'.

Many of the items we now consider to be kitchen furniture, such as dressers and Windsor chairs were originally in use in other rooms in the larger house. Conversely, the poor cottage kitchen contained not only the table and stools or chairs, but also the bed, since this room was the only one with any heating. Traditional kitchen furniture, however, usually included flour and dough bins, shelves or dressers, stools, benches and chairs, and tables.

Flour collected from the mill was still in a rough state and needed sifting to shake out husks and dirt. A flour boulter looks like a chest of drawers with a top which can be raised. The meal was poured into the top on to a sloping platform, and filtered on to a brush inclined at an angle. The refined flour fell through to the bottom 'drawer' and discarded material came out of a small chute at the side. The two top drawers are in fact dummies. With this method of sifting the flour, it was reckoned that about 4 lb more flour was obtained from 2 bushels of wheat than if the flour had been refined at the mill, and this was a considerable saving for poor families.

A wooden dough trough, usually roughly made of pine, was an essential adjunct to breadmaking. The earliest form, called a dough tray, was an oblong box with a lid. It was important that the box could be easily moved to a warm place to help the dough rise. Accordingly, the ends were often carved with extended handles. When legs were added, the tray became a trough. On many troughs the lid was not joined to the box, and those lids with handgrips were turned over to form a breadboard for kneading. Most dough troughs are very plain, although the Pennsylvania Dutch liked to paint them to match the rest of their decorated kitchens. Towards the end of the nineteenth century dry sinks were also popular, and these were designed like the bottom of a dresser, with a hollow box on top and a lid which could be used as a breadboard. When commercially baked bread was available, many homes made do with smaller dough risers. At the end of the nineteenth century dough risers were often made of heavy tin, like a deep pan with a domed perforated lid to allow room for the dough to rise. A rolled rim at the top of the pan allowed the cover to rise as well if necessary.

Pennsylvania Dutch poplar dough trough painted with tulips, late 18th century. The lid could be reversed to provide a surface for kneading.

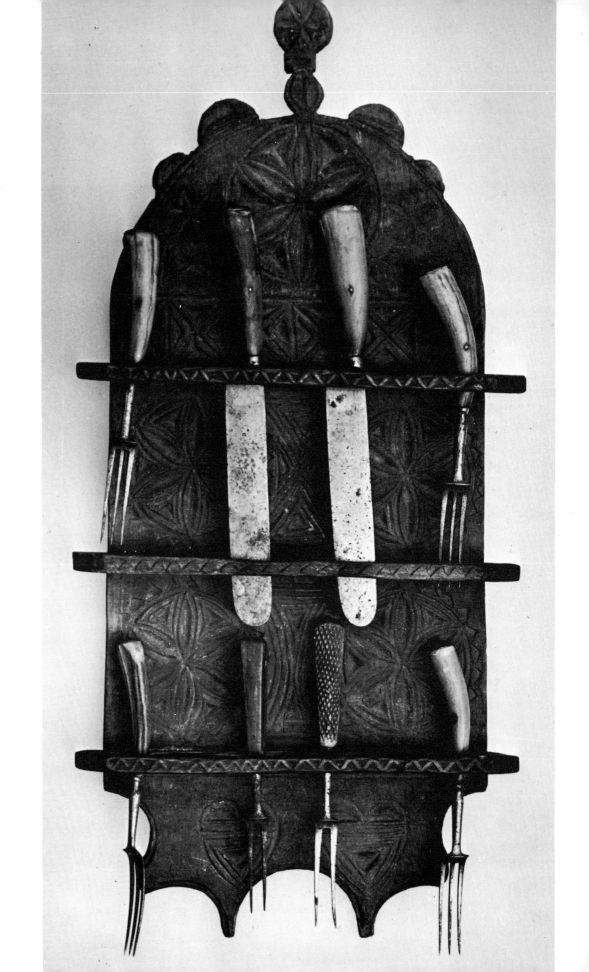

Left Pennsylvania Dutch cutlery rack made in poplar wood with carved decoration, mid-18th century

Pieces of cutlery were precious possessions and in order to keep them clean and dry they were stored near the fire. Spoons, and sometimes knives and carving forks were placed in a spoon rack attached to the wall. Sometimes there was a small drawer underneath the rack, and this was used for spices and seasonings, or precious pieces of small equipment. These cupboards may be flat to hang on the wall or triangular to fit into a corner. They are often heavily carved or painted, with decorative hangers, or bases supporting a small shelf for a piece of china, and most have a lock and key. Very occasionally these hanging cupboards have a matching piece of corner furniture designed to stand beneath them.

The American pie safe seems to be a direct descendant of the Elizabethan livery cupboard. Livery cupboards were either mounted on legs, or were made to hang on a wall. The front and sides were pierced with ventilation holes, or made of turned balusters set close together.

Right Pennsylvania Dutch walnut hanging cupboard fitted with lower drawer and rail, and decorated with incised tulip motifs, 1772

Sometimes the cupboard was surmounted by a canopy. The livery was bread, wine or beer, which each person took to his room at night together with candles. The food was generally placed in the cupboard and the drink on top.

The pie safe used by the Pennsylvania Dutch was made with a wooden frame and top; it was mounted on legs, and sometimes contained a base drawer. The doors and sides were covered with decoratively punched tin or zinc panels, and the inside shelves were used for storing baked goods and pies. The frames were often painted in bright colours and decorated, and there were usually two doors for easy access. Sometimes the four supporting corner posts of the pie safe were extended above the top so that the safe could be hung from cellar beams, and the food was kept away from any rising damp.

The kitchen dresser was originally a side table on which meat and fish were dressed or prepared before cooking. An Essex inventory of 1727 referred to this side table as a dresser board, by which time the original table had acquired doors and drawers. It was common practice to put shelves on the wall above this table, and eventually the shelves and table with drawers became joined as a dresser. Instead of preparing food on this piece of furniture, the housewife began to use it as a storage place, and 'dressed' or decorated the shelves with her best pewter and china. The original type of dresser with a table top and drawers is sometimes called a tavern table in America, although the tables used in taverns and inns were generally smaller and lighter without drawers so that they could be easily stacked.

Dresser designs vary from the most primitive to the highly decorated, and there are many regional variations. The most simple dressers were made of pine with a set of shelves arranged above a single cupboard. Dressers which were brought to England by the Flemish refugees usually incorporate elaborate carving, and sometimes a spoon rack in place of shelves. This style was also used by the Pennsylvania Dutch in America. The traditional Welsh dresser has drawers in the lower parts, although some from South Wales also have cupboards. A few dressers from Merioneth (North Wales) have small doored compartments on either side of the shelves. In the North of England dressers combine drawers and cupboards, but many Yorkshire ones have a plate rack with guard rails, separate from the dresser below. In the North Country and East Anglia, these shelves are still known as 'Delft Racks', an allusion to the plates which were arranged upon them. Some North Country and Midland dressers have bobbined galleries on the shelves, and these are said to be derived from a type of dresser found in Brittany. Later designs became increasingly elaborate, with cabriole legs and inset clocks, but these more properly belonged to the dining room. The kitchen dresser became more functional by the middle of the nineteenth century, and doors were fitted to cover the shelves on the upper part, as a first step to the new hygienic kitchen and the built-in unit.

Oak cupboard with pierced decoration in the door, to allow air to circulate; Welsh, 15th century

Pennsylvania Dutch plate rack with heart and star design and scalloped edges, 18th century

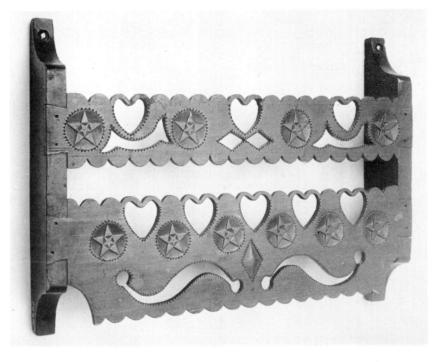

The earliest tables were solid plain affairs of oak or elm, consisting of loose boards (sometimes called planks) on trestles or 'horses'. As early as the thirteenth century, however, some tables were known as 'dormants', being the first permanent tables made with solid ends joined by a single stretcher, but these did not come into common use until the early seventeenth century. They were normally rectangular and joined, i.e. with the frames mortised and tenoned, and the joints secured with wooden pegs.

In Colonial America the table top or board was made of a single plank of the widest available wood, or of two or three planks held together by batten strips on the underside or at each end. These were often known as 'breadboards'. A type of American table popular with the eighteenth-century Pennsylvania Dutch had X-crossed legs and a single stretcher, and was known as a 'sawbuck' table. Earlier settlers also used tables with X-crossed legs, which were joined at the centre by a peg, bolt or screw, and were separate from the board top. When not in use in their small houses, the legs were folded and stacked in a corner, and the table board put against a wall. Such table tops were narrow, for they were more commonly used for serving than for sitting down to meals.

In the nineteenth century the kitchen table was firmly built on four legs. Mrs Beeton, doyenne of English cooks, said that a kitchen table should be 'massive, firm and strongly made'. She recommended that the top should be scrubbed clean every day, but the rest should be painted or varnished. Another type of Victorian table had a large slab of marble inset in the top for rolling pastry and preparing sweet-

33

Above Pennsylvania Dutch oak sawbuck table with X-legs and single stretcher, mid-18th century

Right Hutch-table or table-chair combining seat, table top and storage box, of the type used in England in the 17th century. This example comes from Old Sturbridge Village in America.

meats. Unfortunately the marble frequently broke, especially if the table was being moved to another house, and thus examples still in good condition are scarce.

The hutch table was a useful piece of adaptable furniture, sometimes known in England as a table-chair. This table is a combination of work top, seat and storage box. The storage box, which was mounted on legs, could be used as a seat when the round table top was swung back out of use to form a seat back. The arms of the seat formed a support for the table top when it was needed.

Until the early seventeenth century there were few chairs, and these were only for important people such as the master of the house. A hard stool or bench was the common form of seat. The traditional stool had a circular seat with three legs, while the bench was constructed like a table, and consisted of a plank mounted on a separate stand. A few stools incorporated the more comfortable saddle-seat of the Windsor chair, but by the mid-seventeenth century the majority were fitted with a gently sloping back for greater comfort.

A variation of the bench was the settle with a high back and an arm at either end. This was made to accommodate three or four people, and was placed with one end against the wall on either side of the kitchen fireplace. An American version of this had a central arm rest and a chest below the seat. The American water-bench looks like a settle, but has a narrower top, made to support buckets of water, and above this there are often a number of storage shelves.

Early chairs were extremely uncomfortable, with either a triangular seat, or a simple box seat with solid arms and a tall back. By the early seventeenth century chairs with more comfortable cane or bass seats were introduced, as were wicker chairs. Rush-bottomed chairs, with or without arms, usually with ladder backs, and often stained black or red, were recorded shortly before 1700. It is thought that these ladderback chairs were introduced from the Netherlands. Early examples have low backs with two or three horizontal splats, and later ones may have five or more splats. Sometimes the top rail and splats may have a shaped outline, while the legs may have ball feet, or a turned stretcher between them.

The Windsor chair, however, was probably the most popular for kitchen use, although the more elaborate varieties were used in other parts of the house as well. J. C. Loudon in his book *Encyclopaedia of Cottage, Farm and Villa Architecture and Furniture,* published in 1833, described the traditional construction of this type of chair.

The Windsor Chair is one of the best kitchen chairs in general use in the midland counties of England. The seat is of elm, somewhat hollowed out; the outer rail (bow) of the back is of ash, in one piece, bent to the sort of horseshoe form shown, by being previously heated or steamed; its ends are then inserted in two holes bored through the seat, and are wedged firmly in from the underside. An additional support is given to the back, by two round rails (sticks), which are also made fast in two holes, formed in a projecting

35

Shaker ladderback chair in curly maple wood from New Hampshire, with three splats and wool webbing seat; American, mid-19th century

part of the seat. These chairs are sometimes painted, but more frequently stained with diluted sulphuric acid and logwood; or by repeatedly washing them over with alum water, which has some tartar in it; they should afterwards be washed over several times with an extract of Brasil wood. The colour given will be a sort of red, not unlike that of mahogany; and by afterwards oiling the chair and rubbing it well, and for a long time, with woollen cloths, the veins and shading of the elm will be rendered conspicuous. Quicklime slacked in urine, and laid on the wood while hot, will also stain it of a red colour; and this is said to be the general practice with the Windsor chair manufacturers in the neighbourhood of London.

Another style described by Loudon was the Scroll Windsor. This was of plainer design, and had a seat in the Windsor pattern, but a different type of back, consisting of two side uprights mortised into the seat. The legs were put together by dowels, as in the Windsor.

The Windsor chair made its appearance in the first quarter of the eighteenth century, and by 1730 John Brown of St Paul's Churchyard, London, was advertising 'all sorts of Windsor Garden Chairs, of all sizes, painted green or in the Wood'—i.e. self-coloured. The chairs were usually painted in black or green, or stained, as they were made of a number of different woods. Self-coloured chairs, left in the unpolished state, were cleaned by scouring with sand.

The seat of a Windsor chair is usually referred to as a saddle-seat, the upper surface being 'dished' or hollowed to accommodate the sitter comfortably. The chair-back was sometimes strengthened by two sticks running diagonally from the yoke-rail down to a small supporting tongue or tail-piece, which was an extension of the main seat. These chairs are often called 'brace-backs'. On the earlier and more comfortable chairs the back sticks are slightly bowed.

The very earliest Windsor chairs do not have bow backs, but have plain straight sticks topped by a plain or ornamental cresting. These are known as 'comb-backs', and when splayed as 'fan-backs'. Many backs included a wide strengthening splat, which became a decorative part of the chair when carved in such patterns as wheels, crowns, urns and Prince-of-Wales feathers. The earlier chairs are braced by H-shaped stretchers, and while the legs are often simple, they can also be very very elaborately turned. Rockers were occasionally added, and often the legs appear to have been cut down when the rockers were fitted.

Windsor chairs were very popular in America, but not only in the kitchen or on the porch. George Washington and Thomas Jefferson both used these chairs in other rooms in their houses. Some early chairs were imported from England, but were quickly copied by the colonists. In 1757 George Washington ordered 'one doz'n strong Chairs of about fifteen shillings price' to be sent from England, and gave exact measurements of the bottoms and details of three different colours to suit the papers of three of the bedchambers. By 1767 John Biggard, a turner of Charles Town, introduced the local manufacture of Windsor chairs 'as cheap as any imported'.

The American chair followed the general pattern of the English Windsor, but with individual variations, such as the addition of a writing stand to Jefferson's chair. Philadelphia claims to be the first town to have produced this type of chair commercially, so that it is often known as the Philadelphia chair. In general, the American chair does not incorporate the wide splat, and the legs are set nearer to the centre of the seat and splayed at a more acute angle than the English product. In addition, there is a tendency to prolong the curve of the back-bow forward to take the curve of the arms in one piece. The stick-backs developed into bow-backs after the middle of the eighteenth century, and in the nineteenth century these two patterns were gradually displaced, and the back was filled with vertical sticks between splayed uprights, crowned by a narrow top-rail.

Benjamin Franklin is credited with the introduction of the American rocking chair. Like the English chairs, these were static chairs mounted on wooden rockers, but the rocker became most popular in the middle of the nineteenth century with the Boston Rocker. This had a distinctive 'roll' seat instead of the saddle-seat, rolled arms and a heavily crested stick-back, which provided a more graceful and comfortable chair.

Traditional bow-back Windsor chair with elaborate splat and cowhorn stretcher; English, early 19th century

Overleaf Butter-making class at Wickham Market, Suffolk, late 19th century. On the right of the picture is a barrel churn, and on the left a butter-worker, which was used to extract surplus moisture from the butter.

3 The Dairy

Most farms and large country houses had a dairy, but even small households kept a cow. This was often provided by the local farmer, and returned to him when dry, so a goat was kept to supplement the milk supply. Cows were kept in towns even in the early part of the twentieth century, and people were used to having fresh milk, cream and buttermilk, and to the preparation of curds and whey, butter and cheese.

The dairy was separate from the kitchen, and was often a detached building, facing north and sited near trees for coolness. Tiered shelves ran round the walls to hold utensils, and nineteenth-century dairy rooms were elaborately tiled for cleanliness and to keep them cool. It was fashionable on very large estates to build beautiful ornamental dairies, often equipped with porcelain dishes and jugs. A notable Chinese Dairy was designed for Woburn Abbey by Henry Holland, and a Royal Dairy was built under the direction of the Prince Consort in 1860 on the Home Farm at Frogmore, near Windsor Castle. A pretty Victorian dairy built in 1870 has been preserved at Easton Park Farm, Woodbridge, Suffolk.

The main function of the dairy was to produce butter and cheese, and methods differed according to the equipment available and regional custom. On a large farm, butter was made once or twice a week. The fresh milk was allowed to settle in bowls, and the cream was skimmed as it rose to the surface. The cream was then agitated in a churn, and it might be many hours before the butter separated from the buttermilk. The butter had to be washed, beaten and worked to remove surplus liquid, and after weighing, it was shaped with pats and sometimes printed with an ornamental marker. Butter which was salted for a long period of storage was packed into a large butter pot or tub.

Cheese-making was a much more complicated affair. The milk had to be heated in large cheese kettles, or in a vat with a hot-water jacket. After the addition of rennet the milk was poured into wooden tubs with covers. When curds formed they were cut in to bean-sized pieces and then reheated until the whey ran out. The dry curds were ground and pressed into muslin-lined vats, covered with a heavy lid, and finally stored in a special cheese cupboard or in a small room upstairs in the farmhouse.

Milking stools may vary slightly in design. The most common type of stool has a seat which is square at the front and supported on two

Opposite The magnificent kitchen at Lanhydrock House, Cornwall, with fully-laden dressers and a huge preparation table. In the background is a linen press on a stand.

Overleaf Storage tins and jars on a window sill in the stillroom at Saltram House, Devon. The glass objects in the foreground are wasp traps.

legs. The back of the seat is curved and supported on one leg, so that the stool may be easily tilted forward. Occasionally a stool is found with a square seat and four legs. Two legs are set at the outer front edges, but the back legs are set a few inches in towards the centre—again, to enable the stool to be tilted forward. A few examples have completely round seats.

After milking into a bucket the dairymaid transferred the milk to wide bowls or tubs in the dairy for butter- and cheese-making. When milk was carried to the house, however, it was often contained in a metal-bound wooden pitcher, narrowing at the top and with a handle set high on the side. Tin or enamel milk cans were smaller containers which could be carried into the fields. The traditional English milk can is cylindrical with a close-fitting lid and a swing handle. The milk can used in the Channel Islands is a more rounded form with a short neck, a flat lid with a lifting loop, and a side handle. A variation on this is the Welsh St David's can, in which the cylindrical sides taper up towards the neck.

The milk was removed from the tubs with heavy wooden spoons or ladles, which have carved hooked ends to hang on the side of the container. Churn scoops and skimming spoons have very short handles with a hook which is often squared off at the end so that the hook and handle together form a steady support when the spoon is placed on a flat surface. Skimming spoons may be identified by their wide pierced bowls. Tin, copper or brass ladles were not used in the dairy, but belonged to the milkmen serving milk straight from the churn.

Some dairies were fitted with lead trays like shallow sinks, into which the milk was poured so that the cream could rise. The milk was then run off, and the cream scraped from the tray for butter-making. More often the milk was poured into wide milk pans which are shallow and have widely flaring sides. These pans were usually made in earthenware,

Wooden milk scoops with hooked handles to hang on the side of the churn; Welsh, 19th century

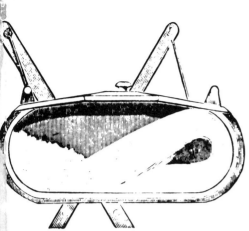

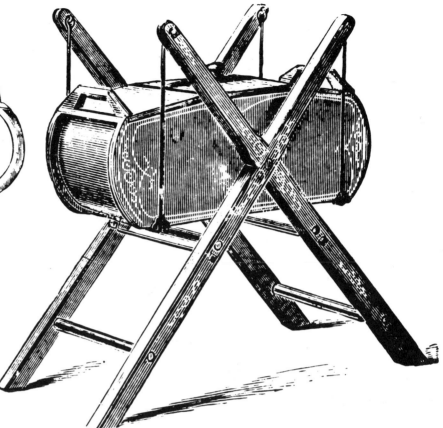

Above and right A sophisticated version of the rocker churn, which could be swung backwards and forwards to agitate the cream

Left Copper ladles and a variety of heavy metal ice-cream and butter moulds at Saltram House, Devon

but glass and marble ones are known. Butter bowls, however, are made of hardwood and are simple hollowed-out circles. These were used for working the butter and kneading it with salt. Cream for the butter was scooped from the milk pans with a shallow perforated ladle called a fleeter.

The action of agitating the cream to form butter was accomplished in a churn, of which there are a variety of forms. The most simple form is the wooden swinging churn. This consists of a hollowed-out bowl with side handles and a conical lid. The churn is suspended by strings attached to the handles, and the whole contraption swings to and fro to agitate the cream.

The most commonly used type was the plunger churn, known in Scotland as the plump churn. This is a tall narrow cylinder of wood, bound with either wooden or metal hoops and fitted with a flat lid. Through the centre of the lid runs a tall handle like a broomstick, fitted at the base with perforated plunger discs. The operator worked this handle up and down and had to toil for many hours to make the butter 'come'. Sometimes this churn was made from a barrel and a development of this style was made in earthenware, looking like a large single-handled jug, or a cylinder with two lugs.

A different churning action was achieved by the rocker churn, which came in three forms. The most simple type was made in wood, shaped

Far left Wooden plunger churn bound with wood; American, late 19th century

Left English stoneware plunger churn, a variation on the earliest wooden type

Below The butter-worker was used to extract moisture from the butter. The grooved wooden roller was worked over the butter, and the excess liquid ran down the sloping tray and could be drained off.

Left Wooden barrel churn, sometimes called an end-over-end churn. The barrel was turned by hand to thicken the cream, and it took about 40 minutes to make butter by this method.

like a baby's cradle on carved rockers, and could be rocked with the foot while sitting. Another form was a lidded oval tub, which was pushed backwards and forwards on a grooved stand. The most sophisticated churn was an oval tub suspended on a stand by metal rods, so that the tub could swing easily backwards and forwards.

The wheel churn could produce large quantities of butter without effort from the dairymaid. The large churn was shaped like a barrel, and fitted with paddle dashers, which were turned by means of a large wheel or circular platform driven by a small dog, or sometimes by water power from a hill stream.

Another form of churn was the box paddle churn with the paddle fitted into a box and turned by a handle. This developed into the barrel churn (sometimes known as the end-over-end churn), which was popular with the dairymaids as it required less effort than the old

Wooden butter stamps and mould, decorated with patterns peculiar to Gloucestershire, a butter spoon and Scotch hands for shaping pats of butter; English, 19th century

48

Above and right Pennsylvania Dutch wooden butter prints with wheatsheaf and tulip motifs, 19th century

plunger churn. The barrel was fitted on to a strong wooden stand, the lid clamped on firmly, and the whole barrel turned for the cream to thicken, which only took 30 to 45 minutes by this method. Glass churns with paddles fitted on the lid are sometimes found, but these are usually small and were only used by the housewife to make small quantities of butter in the kitchen.

Before butter was ready to be made into pats, it had to be pressed and worked to get rid of excess moisture. This was usually done in a butter-worker, which is a shallow curved tray mounted on a stand. The tray is fitted with a spiral rolling pin, which can be turned by a handle. As the roller moves over the butter, the moisture runs down the curve of the tray and into a drain. Butter-makers' tables might also be used for working the butter. These may be found with either three or four legs, and the table tops are in the shape of a flatiron. Like other butter-making equipment these tables were made of alder wood, which is almost completely waterproof.

To prepare butter for market or table, a pair of butter hands or Scotch hands was used. These are two wooden bats with deeply grooved blades about 6 inches long and 4 inches wide. With a bat in each hand the worker could form butter into squares or balls, making a line pattern and zig-zag patterns with the serrated ends of the grooves. Butter was finally finished with a pattern made by a butter stamp. These carved stamps are sometimes mounted on handles, or are fitted inside a container. The butter was pressed into the container, and then ejected by a plunger, which bears a carved design. Another type of stamp incorporates a roller for marking a pattern on a large piece of

Pennsylvania Dutch punched tinware
mould for cream cheese, 1850

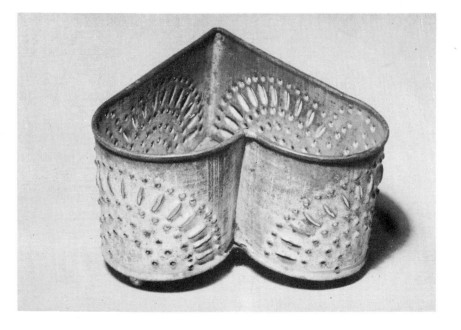

butter. Designs included birds, leaves and flowers. The Pennsylvania
Dutch in America were particularly fond of a tulip motif. Many of the
patterns indicated the place where the butter was made—a valley
farm might use a stamp showing a swan and bulrushes; a hill farm might
have a spray of bog myrtle, and a really good herd would proudly
display butter stamped with the portrait of a prize-winning cow.

Butter had to be weighed before marketing, and special butter scales
were used. These consisted of a simple turned central stand or pillar
with a wooden beam pivoted on a round iron peg. Wooden bowls or
platters were suspended from the ends of the beam.

Soft curd dishes and soft cream cheeses were very popular, and were
shaped in curd moulds. A china three-tiered perforated mould was

Staffordshire glazed mould for making
curd cheese; English, 19th century

filled with curds made by combining fresh buttermilk and milk still warm from the cow. This was well mixed and then extra milk from the next milking was added. The curds were moulded for about an hour, then turned out and served with a sprinkling of powdered sugar and spice. Another form of curd mould is made in tin, in the shape of a heart or star, punched with a pattern of holes. The soft curd cheese was left until solid, turned out and served with fresh cream.

When curds had been prepared for hard cheese, they were pressed into oak tubs or cheese vats lined with muslin. The muslin was folded over the cheese, and a heavy lid or follower placed on top. The cheese remained in the vat for the first night, and then the cheese vats were fitted under the press. To prevent two or more cheeses from sticking together, a large round perforated board with a handle, known as a shooter board, was placed between the vats.

The most primitive form of cheese press incorporated a very heavy stone supported on a frame or stand. A screw at the top of the frame adjusts the height and pressure of the stone, which runs between grooves in the frame. An early example of 1720 is made in wrought steel. A weighted arm can be raised to operate a ratchet, which turns the centre wheel and lowers the press. A later model, dated 1800, has a wrought-iron frame with a screw thread, to which is attached a pinewood disc to press down on to the circular cheese. The cheese vat or mould used with this type of press was made of barrel staves with brass bands and fitted with two handles.

Wooden balances for weighing butter

4 The Laundry

In early days, family linen was washed communally in the local stream. Sometimes a 'battling stone' was set into the bank for beating the washing clean, but in more sophisticated communities an open-sided wash-house was built beside the stream to accommodate the village women. Examples of such wash-houses are still in use in some parts of France. When hot water was needed, an iron cauldron was heated on an open fire. This later developed into an outside brick-built hearth in the courtyard of cottages, and gradually extensions were built on to even small houses to enclose the fire and a built-in cauldron or copper. In the nineteenth century working-class town and village families continued to use communal wash-houses, which were built beside the lavatory and bakehouse, and which might serve the needs of as many as twenty families. In large houses a team of laundry maids worked from 4 o'clock in the morning on wash day to cope with the family wash, but smaller households managed with a visiting washerwoman.

Washing was traditionally prepared on Saturday at the end of the working week, when heavily-soiled clothes were left to soak during Sunday, and white and coloured clothes were separated. Dirty spots were rubbed with a flour paste, which was thinned with a little hot water.

Early washing equipment was extremely simple and little has survived since so much of it was made in wood. In George Washington's wash-house at Mount Vernon equipment consisted of 9 tubs, 4 pails, 2 piggins (small wooden pails with extended handles), 4 tables, 2 boilers and 1 wooden horse.

Washtubs were commonly made by the local cooper, and were often identical to those made for the brewer or dyeworks. The water was heated in an iron cauldron. Sometimes this flanged round utensil was made in copper, and at Mount Vernon it was heated on a brick stove. This type of cauldron gave its name to the copper, which was then built in over the fire, and in later days became an electrically heated container for washing.

Early washing preparations were made by hand, and lye (made from wood ash) was mixed with household grease to make a type of soap. Lye on its own, however, was considered superior to washing soda as it did not harm the clothes. The lye dropper was a wooden box about 9 inches high with holes in the base. This was placed over the washtub

An American advertisement for Mrs Partington's Washing Machine, which consisted of a scrubbing device used with the traditional washtub and board

and a layer of twigs arranged in the base of the dropper. Over this was placed a muslin cloth and the wood ash was then put into the dropper. Water was poured through the ash to obtain the alkaline liquid for washing. Oak ashes produced the strongest solution, but apple tree wood was thought to produce the whitest wash.

In the washtub clothes were rubbed against a long paddle-shaped washboard, which had a corrugated surface, and was made of wood, glass or metal. A board patented in the 1830s was advertised as saving soap and as having a 'sanitary front drain'. Any heavily soiled articles were first pounded and rotated in the tub with a wash dolly, sometimes called a peggy-stick, dolly-pin, dolly-peg or chump dolly. This looked like a small four-legged stool attached to an upright handle about 3 feet long, and finished with a cross handle at the top. Sometimes a wash punch was used. This was similar to a dolly, but instead of a stool had a small barrel-like cylinder at the lower end, with segments cut out at the bottom to grip the washing. To serve the same purpose there was also a perforated copper cone on a long handle, called a posser or posher.

After using the dolly and the washboard the laundry maid put the washing into the copper for boiling, and a dolly stick was used for lifting the wash. Finally, after rinsing and wringing out the water, she put the washing onto a drying line, securing it with cleft wooden pegs, which were often made by gipsies. Stockings were dried on a stocking board, shaped like a foot and leg, and tied to the line with strings. A china sock dryer, shaped like a hollow foot, was also used.

Wooden lye dropper; English, c. 1860. Before detergents and soap powders were available, clothes were washed with an alkaline solution called lye, which was obtained by pouring water over wood ash placed in the lye dropper.

Wash dolly (with legs), wash punch, washboard, and wooden stocking boards; English, 19th century

54

A lever-operated wooden washing machine and mangle made in Keighley, Yorks. Note the washboard design and dolly pegs inside and the drainage tap underneath.

Washing could also be dried or aired indoors on a slatted wooden rack, which was fitted with a pulley to draw it up to the ceiling.

Many inventors set their minds to designing a machine to overcome the drudgery of washday. In 1780 an Englishman called Rodger Rodgerson filed a patent for 'an entirely new machine called a laundry for the purpose of washing and pressing of all sorts of household linen, wearing apparel and other things, in a much less expensive and laborious and expeditious manner than any hitherto practiced'. Similar devices were being developed in Europe, and in 1797 American Nathaniel Briggs issued a patent for a machine for washing clothes.

These early machines were based on the principle of friction, and incorporated mechanical versions of the traditional dollies and scrubbing boards. An American washer, patented in 1805, consisted of a tub inside which was a board attached to a lever. The board was pressed down on top of the clothes and worked in a jerky motion to rub the washing against the corrugated base of the tub.

Most machines were worked by cranks or by a rocking cradle motion, but there were one or two exceptions. The Cataract washer, created by John Schull in America in 1831, consisted of two cylinders, fitted one inside the other so that the inner one could be revolved. The Housewife's Darling, however, had only one moving part, which rubbed and squeezed the fabric. Following the appearance of a wringing machine in 1847, and a roller wringer in 1859, yet another washing machine was patented in America, but this was unsuccessful because it tangled and shredded the clothes

In England J. Picken of Birmingham advertised a patent washing machine in 1858. This consisted of a barrel or metal drum, fitted inside with paddles, and mounted on a stand. It worked on the same principle as the rotating butter churn. The washing was placed in the barrel and hot water was poured in. The lid was screwed on, and when a handle was turned the barrel rotated so that the paddles kept the washing moving. Bradford & Co. of London displayed a similar model at the Paris Exhibition in 1867, and this type of machine was still available up to 1907. A variation of the 'churn' machine was made by the Torpedo Washers Company in Huddersfield in 1860, and this was fitted with a conical lid, making the whole machine resemble a torpedo.

In the 1880s there came on the market another type of machine, consisting of a coopered tub with a wooden agitator post, which acted as a mechanical dolly peg. A mangle, which could be turned by a gear handle, was fixed above the tub. A curious lever-operated rocking tub was also available, and this consisted of a watertight wooden box fastened to rockers and fitted inside with corrugated boards. The box was filled with soapy water and the lid was clamped on. As the laundress rocked it up and down the agitating motion loosened the dirt from the clothes. The C.V.S. machine made in Keighley incorporated a mangle on this model.

Development in America was on slightly different lines. The Metro-

55

politan washing machine of 1861 contained an agitator, which stamped out the dirt. The stamping principle was also incorporated in the 1861 Nonpariel machine. This was operated by turning a crank and was fitted inside with 'shoes', which knocked out the dirt. This machine, however, could only treat one garment at a time. In England Mc-Alpines Patent Washing Machine, made by Manlove, Alliott & Co. of Northampton, was said to be based on the old 'stamping mill' used by Cornish tin miners. This was particularly recommended for tackling such items as blankets and counterpanes, and the advertisement emphasised that garments could be washed, boiled and rinsed in the same vessel. The American Doty Clothes Washer available at the same time reverted to the old washboard action, and consisted of a tub with corrugated side walls and bottom. The tub was supplied with a fluted rolling pin to help remove the dirt from the washing. The scrubbing-board action was still being used in the wheel-operated Lone Star washer of 1904.

The Boss hand-operated washing machine made by Huenefeld Co. of Cincinnati, and patented in 1901

A gasoline-operated washing machine made by Maytag Company of Iowa in 1914

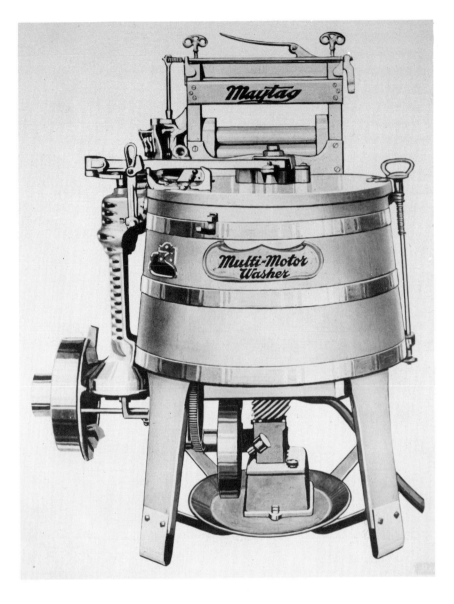

Further developments in America included the Gravity Washer of 1900. This machine incorporated a lid fitted with fins, and the lid could be rotated backwards and forwards by a crank. A more compact agitator attached to the lid was known as the Milk Stool washer, and both this model and the Gravity Washer could be worked from a sitting position. The Maytag Pastime washer of 1907 consisted of a hand-operated wooden dolly, but in 1909 a belt and pulley mechanism was added so that the machine could be operated by means of an outside power source. In 1911 this model was adapted to make use of electricity, and in 1914 a Maytag multi-motor gasoline engine washer was available for homes without electricity.

The Oxford English Dictionary records that the word *mangle* first appeared in the English language in 1774. As early as 1696, however,

Bradford's Improved 'Premier' box mangle illustrated in a 19th-century trade catalogue. The washing was wrapped round the rollers, and the weighted box was cranked backwards and forwards over the rollers. The machine was so heavy that it was usually worked by a man.

the Duchess of Hamilton received a mangle from her cousin, the Countess of Rothes. This cost £53 (Scots), and was sent to Edinburgh with the wheelwright, who was to show the laundrywomen how it worked. According to a late eighteenth-century housekeeping book a mangle was not originally used to express water from the washing, but was used to iron household linen smooth. In a large house the washing was folded on Wednesday to be mangled on Thursday or Friday, and a man was usually employed to work the heavy machine, although this might be done by two maids.

Plain brown Holland mangling cloths, supplied by the mangle maker, were wrapped around the clothes before they were passed through the rollers. These cloths were seldom washed as this spoiled the shining polish which they gave to the household linen. Brown Holland cloths were considered vastly superior to 'common Irish linen' for giving the correct finish, and with careful handling could last up to thirty years.

The box mangle was invented in the eighteenth century, and consisted of two thick cylindrical wooden rollers placed crosswise on the bed of the mangle. The rollers were weighted down by a strong wooden box filled with stones. This was geared so that a man could crank the

Above The Villa domestic mangle was made by Harper & Twelvetrees Ltd, England, in 1870. The pressure of the rollers could be adjusted by the screw on top.

Right Carved wooden mangle bat; Welsh, dated 1669. Wet clothes were wound round a wooden roller, which was then rolled to and fro with the bat to extract the water. The bat could also be used to remove creases from dry or damp items. Most examples were plain and undecorated, but painted and carved bats, such as this one, were often intended as gifts or love tokens.

box backwards and forwards across the rollers underneath, and the weight of the box squeezed out water from the washing. A model in use at Shugborough Hall, Staffordshire was also used for pressing clothes. Small pieces of washing were folded inside larger pieces, such as sheets or tablecloths, and were then wrapped round one of the wooden rollers which fitted under the weighted box of the mangle. Only two rollers were mangled at any one time while a third roller was being clothed. The Shugborough Hall mangle was made by Baker of London in 1810, and was in use until the 1920s. Kent's Double Action Box Mangle was displayed at the London Exhibition in 1862, and was advertised as being lighter, quicker and easier to use.

The box mangle was suitable only for large houses or communal laundries, and during the nineteenth century the housewife was introduced to the domestic wringing or mangling machine. This consisted of two rollers mounted one above the other, and turned by a wheel as the washing was fed through. The whole apparatus could be screwed to the edge of a wooden washtub or placed on a stand. A domestic wringer patented in America in 1847 was said to imitate the action of wringing clothes by hand, but by 1859 models incorporating two rollers were in use. The Villa domestic mangle, made by Harper & Twelvetrees Ltd in 1870, was on a heavy cast-iron stand and the rollers were controlled by a large wheel. The pressure of the rollers was adjusted by a screw, similar in design to that used on a wooden linen press. The Bradford Reciprocal Mangle, available in England, was a lighter model which could be supplied with plain or brass-capped rollers. The more expensive Bradford's Patent Ye Tudor had a combined lever and spring pressure and was decorated with a castellated top. Bradford's also offered lightweight cheap wringers, The Acorn, The Novelty and The Superior, which featured rollers covered with india-rubber. By 1890 Harrods Stores Ltd were offering to re-wood rollers for mangling machines, indicating that the machines had already been in use for some years.

Few cottagers could afford a mangle, and it was common practice to use a mangle bat or battledore. The simple English version consisted of a thick plain piece of oak between 3 and 6 inches wide, shaped like a cricket bat about 3 feet long. Plain clothes were wrapped round a roller, which was then rolled to and fro with the heavy battledore until all creases had gone. The wooden roller and bat could also be used to stir washing in the tub, and was sometimes used like a mangle to push out water from the washing.

These plain battledores do not seem to have survived, but Scandinavian mangle bats have been treasured for generations. These were gaily painted or carved, often with a handle in the shape of a horse. The practice of polishing special ironing with a mangle bat survived in the Royal Navy into the 1920s. The shine of the clothes was improved by placing glossy magazine pages in the folds of suits so that the gloss was transferred from paper to clothes.

A linen press was commonly kept in larger households for finishing table linen. It consisted of a frame and stand with the top crossbar supporting a wooden screw. The screw was controlled by a double handle, which lowered a heavy board under which the cloths could be pressed. This press could be placed on a table or dresser, but at the end of the nineteenth century was supplied with a stand, which was fitted with one or two drawers, and sometimes a cupboard as well. Sometimes the press had no stand, but had its own built-in drawer.

Heavy household linen was normally pressed through a mangle, or rolled with a mangle bat, while table linen was finished in a press. Items finished with a hand iron were known as 'laundry'; the rest was just washing. Ironing was originally done on the kitchen dresser, which was covered with a piece of flannel, but some larger houses had ironing tables fitted along a wall. Intricate ironing was later tackled on skirt boards, sleeve boards and bosom boards.

The hand iron has an ancient history. The Chinese in the eighth century smoothed clothes with a metal object; in the East brass irons with wooden or bone handles were heated with hot coals; while the Viking invaders of Britain used large stones as primitive irons. A further development was the early slickenstone, which looked like a glass mushroom, similar to the type used for darning. It was rubbed over the washing to give it a smooth and shining finish, and continued in use with hatters for smoothing the inside of silk hats.

The flatiron was often known as a 'sadiron' from an old word which meant solid. A simple flatiron was heated on a stand over the fire or on a special stove; the irons were made in pairs with one being heated as the other was used. These were difficult and tiring to use, for the handles were metal, sometimes twisted, and were hot and uncomfortable. The traveller's iron, which was used less frequently, was sometimes fitted with a smooth grooved wooden handle. The 'Enterprise' irons were a set of sadirons with interchangeable handles, patented by Mrs Potts in America in 1871.

Stands for flatirons tend to be more decorative than strictly functional. It seems likely that they were intended as attractive gifts for the good housewife, rather than essential pieces of kitchen equipment. They were made in brass and steel throughout the nineteenth century, and designs varied widely, although the basic stand was in the shape of a flatiron base, supported on three or four feet. Stands ranged in length from about 6½ to 11 inches long, sometimes with an extension of the design forming a handle, and sometimes with an additional turned wooden handle. Many were made in pairs, as more than one iron would be in use as others were being heated.

The most simple design was made in sheet steel with three long peg legs and a triangular pierced stand. A variation on this design was cast in brass, and had heavy peg legs and a pierced star motif. Another heavy brass stand had a fishtail handle and bun feet. Some examples have turned brass feet, while other designs were heavily pierced to give a lacy effect, which would have provided little support for the iron. One or two stands were so elaborately decorated that they are scarcely recognizable as iron-holders. Notable designs include an ornately scrolled solid bronze model; a pierced heart of cut steel with four legs, and a curious stand with a Masonic design of square and compasses, dated 1805 to commemorate the Battle of Trafalgar. A further variation was the highly decorative pierced sheet brass model with three cross partitions, a high pierced gallery and four pierced scroll feet.

Early flatirons needed to be constantly reheated, and in a busy kitchen it was necessary to keep a number of irons heating at the same time. The standard flatiron was heated face down on a hot plate or stove, or propped upright against the fire on a metal stand suspended from the firebars. This contraption was called a 'biddy' in mid-

A selection of 19th-century English irons, including a heavy goose iron (top left), a charcoal iron (top right), a spirit iron, small smoothing irons, and two box irons. The box irons are hollow and have a door at the back of the iron to insert a wedge-shaped piece of brick or iron, which was first heated in the fire.

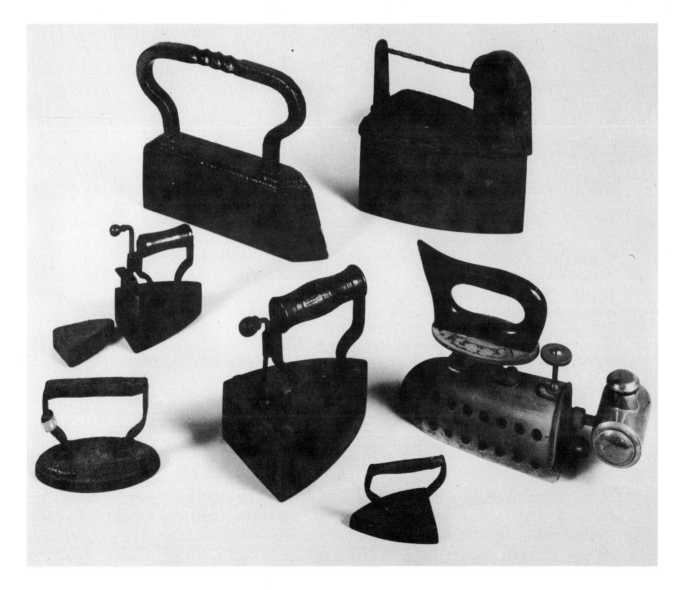

THE AMERICAN MACHINE CO'S.
Crown & Eagle Fluting Machine.   Mrs Potts, Crown Sad Irons.

SOLD HERE.

A variety of crimping irons and fluting machines in use. The advertisement also illustrates Mrs Pott's patent Crown Sad irons with detachable handles.

Staffordshire. Before they could be used the irons had to be cleaned of soot or smoke by rubbing with waxed or brown paper.

Large houses and laundries in the late nineteenth century installed special flatiron stoves, which heated the irons without making them dirty. A firebox was mounted on legs and the smoke was drawn up through a wide box top into a cylindrical chimney. The box top had sloping sides and a base rim to hold the irons. The stoves might be constructed with four wide slopes, each of which would hold two or three irons, or as many as ten sides each holding one iron.

Very heavy irons were used for billiard tables, and irons used by tailors were known as goose irons. The housewife, however, needed something finer than the ordinary flatiron to finish more intricate garments. The lace-iron was particularly small, and the bottom edge was curved to avoid catching threads.

The finishing or tally iron is now often wrongly described as a goffering iron. The process of goffering, or crimping, was carried out

Flatiron heating stove made by
C. Carpenter & Co. of Boston, Mass.
and used in large houses and
commercial laundries at the end of
the 19th century

Finishing or tally
iron and sheath, used
to smooth the edges
of clothes, cuffs and
collars

by other means, and is discussed later in this chapter. The finishing
iron was actually used to smooth the edges of ironed garments, not to
ruffle them. Sometimes called an Italian iron, this was also popular
for smoothing ribbons and bows. These irons were cigar-shaped, and
had long handles. They were heated in the fire and then placed in a
protective metal sheath mounted on a stand. The sheath transmitted
heat, but prevented the clothes from being dirtied by soot and charcoal.
Cuffs, collars and sleeves were passed backwards and forwards over
the sheath to smooth out wrinkles. The same type of sheath was sometimes used to hold heated tongs, which could be used to corrugate
ruffles. The actual irons and tongs are now hard to find, as they were
slender and easily worn away or broken, or put to other household
uses. The protective sheaths, however, may be often found on their own.

Ruffles had to be crimped or goffered. Both processes gave a corrugated finish, but crimping produced a finer and closer effect. Originally
this process was carried out on a goffering stack, which was a wooden

frame about 13 inches high. Wooden quills were slotted horizontally between the two side-pieces of the frame. The damp material was wound round the quills and clamped down by an adjustable top bar. The stack was then put by the fire so that the linen would dry into a corrugated shape. A more elaborate crimping machine was also made in wood and was a frame about 20 inches high, with a roller at the top to hold the material firmly in place. The horizontal bars were arranged in such a way that they form two tiers. The material was wound in between the bars and clamped down by an inverted T-shaped piece of wood, which was slotted into grooves in the side-pieces of the frame. Another version of this stack was fitted with a roller and pulleys at one side to hold surplus material.

Crimping board and roller made from boxwood for gathering and pleating ruffles, which were stitched at the top, and a metal fluting iron, used by dressmakers to crimp material

In the seventeenth and early eighteenth century a crimping board and roller was often used. This consisted of a corrugated boxwood board and a separate grooved roller. The fabric was starched, damped, placed on the board, and crimped by working the roller to and fro. This device was also used for gathering and pleating ruffles, which were then stitched at the top. A development of this was the fluting iron, which worked like a miniature mangle, and had two corrugated rollers to crimp linen. These irons were particularly popular with dress-makers. A simpler type of fluting iron consisted of two four-pronged forks, hinged together at the neck. They were fitted with long handles so that the prongs could be heated in the fire and applied to the frills to crimp them.

Fluting iron; American, c. 1869

64

The original flatirons were tiresome to use as the work had to be done by the fire, and the irons often became sooty and smutty. The first self-heated irons were known as box irons, chimney irons or charcoal irons. The earlier examples were hollow and had a large door at the back of the iron into which was placed a wedge-shaped brick or piece of iron. This had to be heated in the fire and needed careful handling. A later development was the iron into which burning coals or charcoal were placed. In 1862 Kent's of London advertised a Self-Heating Box Iron which could be 'heated at pleasure in three minutes, without any fire, and will remain hot at a nominal cost for any length of time'. A funnel at the front provided ventilation and carried the fumes away. When charcoal was used, it was kept glowing by periodically blowing through the hole in the back, or by opening the door and vigoriously swinging the iron to and fro.

The advent of electricity prompted the invention of cleaner, more efficient irons which did not need constant re-heating. In 1894 the City of London Lighting Co. produced electric irons, but these weighed about 14 lb, and were used only by tailors and hatters. In America an electric flat iron had been invented in 1889 by Mr Carpenter, a restaurant owner of St Paul, Minnesota, following his success in producing an electrically heated griddle for his restaurant. Earlier, in 1882, a Mr Seely had patented an iron on a base heated by an electric current, but this was little better than the old method of heating on a stove, since the iron still had to remain near its heat source. Mr Carpenter's self-heating iron was originally used by a tailor, but by 1896 electric irons for the home were available in America. Development of electric products was slow during the early years, since even the larger electric power companies only supplied electricity at night when lights were needed. In 1902 Earl H. Richardson, superintendent of a small electric generating company in California, supplied electricity on Tuesdays only, and designed an electric iron which was distributed to his customers. A domestic electric iron weighing 8 lb was produced by General Electric at Pittsfield, Mass., in 1904. It was recommended that the user should turn off the iron frequently to 'save electricity', but in reality this was the only method of controlling the heat. By 1913 General Electric advertised a similar model with the new heel-stand on which the iron could be tipped back and rested, obviating the need for a separate iron-stand.

A dangerous experiment in heating was the spirit-iron. A gasoline iron with a fuel container at the rear was patented in America in 1902. A British version of 1907 featured a methylated spirit container at the back with a burner, and was pierced with two rows of holes along the sides. These irons were about as safe as bombs, and soon gave way to electric irons in progressive households.

Gasoline flatiron patented in America in 1902

5 Cleaning the House

Although cleaning the house took up a substantial part of the day for a housewife or her servants, very little of this cleaning equipment has survived. Cleaning methods hardly changed for centuries, and brooms and sweepers were used until they were worn out, and then replaced with similar items. Brushes and containers were strictly utilitarian, and were certainly never treasured for their beauty.

The first sweeping brushes were bundles of twigs or heather bound on to a rough stick. They were bought from travelling broom salesmen or made at home. Brush-making was a traditional winter evening's occupation for farmers; in New England they used birch or ash twigs, while in other areas hickory was popular. The tuft of the maize plant made a very good brush, and this material was utilized by Ebenezer Howard, who in 1859 started the first American brush factory in Montgomery County, New York. Many acres around New York were given over to the cultivation of broom corn, and the brooms were often made by hand in prisons or asylums for the blind.

This type of flat broom, known as the American Pattern, was still in use in England in 1895. Another kind of broom with a rounder head was called the Albert Carpet Broom. Alongside these were sold a different type of broom with bass, bristle or hair tufts set in a wooden holder mounted on a smooth broomstick.

By the end of the nineteenth century there was a great range of brushes available for different purposes. Ostrich-feather dusters were used for light dusting, and banister brushes, with short handles, and sometimes double heads, for cleaning the staircase. Double-ended furniture brushes were used with tin dustpans. Geo. H. Mason of Boston marketed a steel-edged dustpan, which was guaranteed to pick up all dust and dirt and to outlast a dozen of 'the common style'. This was available in the plain enamelled form or 'hand-painted, fancy'.

For special tasks there were wide-angled stove brushes with such names as Porcupine, Double Bent, Kitchener, Eugene, Regent and Wing'd, and special little black lead brushes with turned handles. A set of three brushes—hard, shine and blacking—was used for boot-cleaning, together with a flat and a round boot varnish brush. For other rooms in the house a heavy billiard table brush might be necessary, or the crumb brush with tray to match, elaborately decorated and marketed under the name of The Carlton or The Fluted. Some-

Advertisement for stove polish,
New York, 1878

times these were replaced by brass or copper crumb scoops with matching oval trays known as waiters. Hearth brushes were particularly decorative, and the small brush head was mounted on a long, sometimes telescopic handle made of brass with repoussé decoration, polished oak or ebonized wood.

Brushes and polishes were carried from room to room in the housemaid's box, which was fitted with a short handle. A decorative three-tiered broom stand, with holes to support long brooms and small loops and trays for hand brushes, was also popular in the 1890s.

In view of the spate of inventions in the second half of the nineteenth century it is surprising that so little attention was paid to the many cleaning jobs which had to be tackled by servants or the poorer housewife. As late as 1883 American Laura C. Holloway wrote in *The Hearthstone*:

A handful or two of damp salt sprinkled on the carpet will attract and absorb the dust and carry it along with it, and make the carpet look fresh as new. Wet corn meal is also excellent and serves the same purpose. So do damp cabbage leaves cut up small, if no other means are at hand.

She also recommended shaking and beating a carpet, tacking it firmly to the floor, and then washing it with a clean flannel dipped in a mixture of bullock's gall and cold water.

As early as 1699 a patent had been issued to Edmund Heming for 'a new machine for sweeping the streets of London or any city or town'. This consisted of a large circular brush, mounted on a horsedrawn cart; when the cart moved the brush was rotated by means of gears connected to the wheels. The machine raised clouds of dust and the strenuous protests of the residents. It was not until 1811 that James Hume patented a machine based on the same principles but designed to sweep floors. This was a box equipped with a brush, which was revolved by means of a pulley and string mounted on the broomstick handle. In 1858 Lucius Bigelow designed an improved model, which began to gain popularity in Britain. A similar model was brought out by H. H. Herrick in Boston, but delivery of orders was delayed by the outbreak of the Civil War. The idea spread, however, and models called Weed, Boston, Welcome, Whirlwind and Lady's Friend soon appeared on the market.

The first really effective carpet sweeper was devised by Melville R. Bissell, who constructed a floor sweeper to get rid of straw dust (to which he was allergic) in his china shop in Grand Rapids, Michigan in the 1870s. The model was adapted to sweeping carpets, its main feature being a knob for adjusting the brushes to the surface to be swept. A patent was granted in 1876, and the Bissell Grand Rapids became the most popular carpet sweeper in both America and Britain. Some early sweepers were fitted with 'side whiskers' for cleaning skirting boards.

By 1900 various machines were in use in factories and railway carriages to blow away dust. This method was tried in a few homes, but only succeeded in redistributing the dust. Herbert Booth, an English engineer, decided that the answer was to suck dust into a container, rather than blow it away. He demonstrated this by sucking dust from the plush upholstery of his restaurant chair and from the floor through his handkerchief. In 1901 he patented Booth's Original Vacuum Cleaner Pump—a contraption of pumps and linen, nicknamed 'Puffing Billy'. The first cleaners were massive constructions with electric or petrol-driven pumps mounted on horsedrawn carts. Drawing-room tea parties were held to watch the vacuum cleaner at work.

In America at about the same time, Corrine Dufour of Georgia invented the Electric Sweeper and Dust Gatherer. The mechanism consisted of a rubber roller, which drove a pair of brush cylinders making frictional contact with the carpet. An electric motor in the cleaner hood operated a fan, which picked up dust and dirt and drove it against a sponge saturated with water. The dirty sponge had to be removed for cleaning. This machine, however, met with little success, but a more popular model was devised by an American plumber, David E. Kenny. A nozzle with a slot about 12 inches long and 3/16th inch wide was attached to a metal tube, which also served as a handle. A wide hose connected this handle to a larger pipe, which led to a vacuum pump and filtering devices. In 1901 he applied for patents, which were granted in 1907, and for many years American cleaners could only be made under a Kenney licence.

Early vacuum cleaning continued to be a formidable task, best carried out by a team of men. In America the Connersville Blower Company offered a reward of $1000 to anyone who could devise a portable outfit mounted upon either a motor car or horsedrawn wagon. The invention of a really portable vacuum cleaner became a challenge, and the Hoover Company's museum in Ohio contains models of hundreds of devices which never achieved commercial success. The Hoover family had been a successful firm of saddlers, but with the growing demand for motor cars they began to look for other types of work. In 1907 J. Murray Spangler, a member of the family, produced an electric suction sweeper made of tin and wood with a broom handle and a sateen dust bag. A refined model of the Spangler machine was on the market by 1908, supported by a team of travelling salesmen offering a demonstration and free ten-day trial in the home. The Hoover machine was further developed in 1908 by Francis Mills Case, who recognized the importance of vibrating the carpet to loosen embedded dirt. This particular model combined brisk sweeping action by revolving brushes with strong suction by a fan. Another American, James Kirby of Cleveland, devised a water vacuum cleaner, which was marketed by his Domestic Vacuum Cleaner Company at the high price of $25 without a motor, and $85 with one. He sold his motor repair shop to concentrate on the development of a broomstick model cleaner, and by 1910 he had perfected a device that permitted attach-

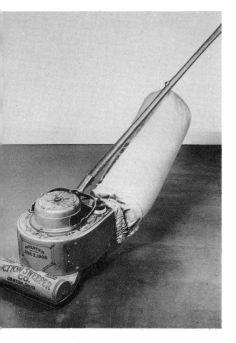

Broomstick model vacuum cleaner, patented by the Electric Suction Sweeper Co of Ohio in 1908

Electrically driven trolley vacuum cleaner, with a dust container and wide variety of accessories, made by the British Vacuum Cleaner Co Ltd in 1906

ments to be connected to the cleaner. Popular broomstick models in America were the Eureka and the Frantz Premier, and in Britain the Daisy and the Magic. A formidable American version was a tank-type cleaner called the Pneumatic. This was connected to a ceiling light outlet, and was advertised in 1906 as being capable of 'drying milady's hair'

An interesting combination of sweeper and vacuum cleaner was the non-electric 1913 Sweeper-Vac made by the Pneuvac Company of Boston. The firm advertised their vacuum carpet sweeper as being suitable for castle or cottage, and said that it would remove from a cupful to a quart of dirt from a rug, even after it was beaten.

The other important cleaning device in the home was the knife cleaner. Steel knives had to be carefully cleaned to remove food stains. Originally they were scoured with a strong solution of common washing soda and water, and then polished on a knifeboard, covered with buff leather or india rubber. Forks were cleaned by the same method. By the end of the nineteenth century two kinds of machine had been developed to speed up the work. Knight's patent knife cleaner resembled a miniature mangle, with a revolving india-rubber roller which 'gives a beautiful silver-like polish to the blades without wearing them away or causing any damage whatever to the handles. From four to eight knives can be cleaned in one minute, shoulders and back included.'

The most common type of knife cleaner was circular in shape. Kent's patent machine, devised in 1882, consisted of a wooden drum mounted vertically on a cast-iron stand. By 1890 Kent's had produced the less-expensive Improved Patent model. Two cheaper versions, the Davis Excelsior, and the Spong Patent Self-adjusting Stag, were highly recommended by Harrods of London.

The knives were slotted into grooves on the side of the drum-shaped container, which was mounted on a stand. An inner wheel, fitted with leather leaves, could be turned by a handle, and this cleaned and stropped the knives. An abrasive emery powder (made by Kent's, Borwick's or Oakey & Sons) was used to assist the process. The knives were dusted free of powder as they were taken from the brush-lined apertures of the machine. Smaller knife cleaners would take only three knives and a carver, but larger models could take up to six knives, and were available on high or low stands.

Knife cleaner made by Spong, and a tin of Oakey's knife polish; English late 19th century

6 Storage and Preservation

The storage of food and other household commodities was of great importance in the days when grain and flesh had to be kept from autumn to spring, and when every scrap of dried fruit, spice and salt was precious. At Hamilton Palace in 1690 the Duchess Anne had a large room with a fireplace to serve as a larder. Rows of barrels for barley, herring and meal were ranged along the walls. There were shelves of little boxes for rice and mustard seed and for dishes of dried fruit, while a miniature chest of drawers contained a variety of spices. Cheese and sugar loaves were also kept on the shelves, and underneath there were wooden chests for storing bread and candles. Pewter trenchers, stone and glass bottles and the family silver were also stored in this room.

An arrangement of storage drawers was still popular in 1776 when Susannah Whatman was housekeeping in Kent. In her Closet Storeroom, she had deep drawers to contain ready-broken sugar.

There is one for spice, one for moist sugar, and two for lump sugar. The pieces should be as square as possible, and rather small. The sugar that is powdered to fill the silver castor should be kept in a bason in one of the drawers to prevent any insects getting into it, and be powdered fine in the mortar and kept ready for use. Currants and raisins should be kept in a moister place, as in the deep drawers in the little cupboard opposite the Storeroom. Rice should be ground at leizure times, and kept for use.

Such storage drawers can still be seen at Inverary castle, home of the Duke of Argyll.

Mrs Sara J. Hale in *The Good Housekeeper* (Boston 1839) was even more specific in her instructions.

Crusts and pieces of bread should be kept in an earthen pot or pan, closely covered in a dry cool place. Keep fresh lard and suet in tin vessels. Keep salt pork fat in glazed earthenware. Keep yeast in wood or earthen. Keep preserves and jellies in glass, or china or stone ware. Keep salt in a dry place. Keep ice in the cellar, wrapped in flannel. Keep vinegar in wood or glass.

During the same period industrious housewives were saving pigs' bladders as containers for lard, and intestines for sausages. Their dried fruit and herbs were stored in home-made paper bags, and butter was

Wooden coffee mill and a tin spice box with six compartments and a nutmeg grater, which fits inside the box

salted and packed into stone jars or oak firkins. Cheeses had to be stored in a dark cool room, and each day turned and rubbed with fat fried out of salt pork. Eggs were stored, with pointed end downwards, in a cool place, or they were packed in a mixture of salt and lime.

Meat and game had to be hung in an airy place, and the traditional meat safe was suspended from the ceiling, or sometimes outside from a tree or a hook. Meat safes were cube-shaped, with a hipped roof, and were made of japanned iron with sides of wire mesh. The safes were fitted with a hook in the centre of the roof, and often incorporated a shelf inside, and a lock on the door. They ranged in size from 16 to 24 inches high, and were sturdily constructed to hold a considerable weight of meat. Domed wire covers on an oval metal base with a central handle were used to cover cooked food or small pieces of raw meat on plates on larder shelves.

Salt-glazed stoneware crocks were used for keeping jams, preserved fruits, salted foods and butter, and liquids such as cider and vinegar. Some were the size of milk churns, but others contained only one or

American cake tin advertising Schepp's Cocoanut, late 19th century, with illustrations relating to Goethe and Schiller. An inscription inside reads: 'Economy and Cleanliness go hand in hand. A good housekeeper is a promoter of happiness. Schepp's Cocoanut is sold on its merits only. Some dealers sell inferior cocoanut claiming it as good as Schepp's. The reason why they do this is because they receive scheme prizes, Etc. Schepp's Cocoanut is used by first class housekeepers who do not care for premiums but prefer quality. A good article is appreciated for what it is.'

Painted tin kitchen security safe for storing flour, spices and other staple foods; American, *c.* 1900. Note the lock in the lower centre panel, and the handle for grinding coffee

Painted tin sugar box and lid, possibly from New York State, 19th century

two pints. The traditional pot has a small lug on either side and a rim over which a bladder or waxed cloth could be securely tied for preservation. The English jars are normally in plain cream or brown earthenware, occasionally with a simple incised decoration. Grey American jars, however, often feature a primitive cobalt blue slip motif of a house, a cow, a bird, a decorative frieze, or even crossed flags, and the impressed name of the maker and his location.

Wooden tubs, hooped with wood and fitted with a knobbed lid, were popular for butter, but were also used for flour. The wooden sugar barrels used by the Pennsylvania Dutch were frequently decorated with coloured patterned bands. Their love of colourful decoration is evident on many of their storage jars and boxes of pottery and tinware. Similar British models are severely plain and functional by comparison, and feature no decoration other than the name of the stored commodity, such as 'flour' or 'sugar'.

For centuries jam, fruit, vegetables and meat had been preserved in jars, which were kept airtight by means of a bladder or a cloth dipped

Opposite South Union Shaker preserve jars, with the labelled top of the wooden crate in which they were packed and a tool for tightening the jar lids

A collection of salt-glazed stoneware storage jars decorated with lively animals, bird and flower designs; American, mid-19th century

in wax or mutton fat. A threaded screw-type glass jar was first patented by John L. Mason of New York in 1858. From 1886 onwards the American company Balls made a variety of preserving jars, the earliest being the Buffalo jar, which had a glass insert at the top with a zinc screwband. Sometimes the jars were made in clear glass, but more often they were aqua green, which helped to keep the colour of the preserve. A further development patented in 1908 was the Ball Sure Seal. The lid of the jar was fastened by a wire bail, known as the Lightning Closure, and sealed by a rubber ring, which fitted inside the glass lid.

Traditional English brown-glazed earthenware storage jars

Right Earthenware salt kit or storage jar with white slip decoration; English, early 19th century

Below Wooden salt box for hanging near the fire to keep the contents dry; English, mid-19th century

Salt was a precious commodity, and for many years was the only means of seasoning food in Colonial America. It was therefore stored carefully in a box or jar, which was hung by the fire to keep the contents dry. The most common type of salt box was made of oak, and had a full-length leather hinge which would not corrode. The boxes usually had a sloping lid and a carved wood backpiece, which was pierced for hanging on the wall. Pennsylvania Dutch examples of the eighteenth century are usually carved or painted as well.

Salt jars were particularly useful as they could be hung up, or could stand by the side of the fire or on a range without damage. They were made in red earthenware and were frequently decorated in primitive white slip patterns under a yellow, blue or green glaze.

Large quantities of spices were used for flavouring and preserving food. The spice was not powdered, but stored whole, and kept dry in a variety of boxes and tins. A miniature chest of labelled drawers was made to stand on a table, or to hang on the wall. By 1840 this had developed into an attractive column of stacking boxes in turned wood.

78

Japanned tin boxes became popular in the nineteenth century, since they were light and easily portable. A simple derivation of the chest of drawers is the oblong tin box with six compartments, each with a labelled lid and small lifting loop. Round boxes with wedge-shaped compartments and a domed lid often have a centre circular section designed to hold a small grater. A more utilitarian type of box was the circular metal tub fitted with a loop handle and containing five or six separate small circular tins with labelled lids. This was available in 1890 in 'art colours'. A simple two-section lidded box is a late Victorian seasoning box, designed to hold salt and pepper for easy use near the fire.

Knives, candles and matches were equally precious items which had to be kept dry. The earliest knife boxes look very similar to salt boxes, but are much deeper. Steel knives were cleaned and placed in the box, which was hung by the fire to keep the blades dry and free from rust. Later knife boxes were wide and flat, with two hinged lids on either side of a carrying handle. In rich households, the best table knives were kept in elegant slotted knife boxes made in highly polished

Black japanned tin spice box with individual hinged containers for six different spices; English, mid-19th century

79

wood. These were kept on the sideboard and were usually locked. Very occasionally a knife box was combined with a spoon rack, often with carved and decorated sides.

Candles were originally kept in clothes chests since tallow was thought to be a preventative against moths. By the eighteenth century candles were kept in simple small chests with sliding wooden lids, and, like so many other storage items, were gaily decorated by the Pennsylvania Dutch. A few were made in pewter or silver. Less attractive but just as practical were the early nineteenth-century tin tubular candle holders with sturdy straps for hanging and a simple hasp to close the lid. This type of candle box continued in use until the end of the century.

In the last half of the nineteenth century, when matches had superseded tinder boxes, these were kept in very decorative little holders, which hung on a wall. Made in tin, cast iron and brass, they were often painted or cast with a decorative pattern.

As early as the eleventh century, ice wells were used by monastic establishments for the preservation of food. Ice houses first made their

English circular metal spice box with a grater; carved wooden nutmeg grater; and a German wooden spice chest

appearance in the middle of the seventeenth century, when many owners of large estates used the winter ice from low-lying ponds to keep specially built ice caves cold. The ice was cut in thick blocks and stored in a brick room either built into a hillside, or the dry bank of a moat, or covered with a roof of insulating thatch. Charles II had an ice house built in St James's Park; most large country houses had one (some were in use until the 1920s), and a few town houses. In America ice from the northern states was shipped to the southern states, and even sent round Cape Horn to San Francisco. Wenham Lake ice was imported from America to Britain for delivery in towns throughout the Victorian era.

Ice-cooled boxes were in use in American homes as early as 1830, but there was confusion over their function. It was thought important to save the ice, which was wrapped in a blanket, thus preserving the ice but not the food. Tin- or zinc-lined boxes were introduced about 1840 to hold ice cut from a lake, or delivered by the ice-man. These ice boxes are about the size of a wooden blanket box and the ice was placed in the bottom of the metal-lined interior, with the food above. The Alaska Ice Chest was still available from Harrods of London in 1890. It was made of ash, lined with zinc and filled with charcoal, but now there were two square lids let into the top, instead of the simple lifting lid of the early blanket-box type.

In the 1850s, however, it was realized that the ice should be at the top of the unit, with air circulating round it. A system based on this principle was patented in 1856, and by 1860 it had been developed to use in a refrigerator. This type of refrigerator, which incorporated a top cabinet filled with pieces of crushed ice and provision for the drainage of melting ice, was marketed until 1914, when it was replaced by refrigerators making artificial ice.

Pennsylvania Dutch painted wooden candle box, late 18th century

In 1755 artificial ice was prepared by Dr William Cullen in Scotland, but like so many potentially useful kitchen inventions this was not fully developed for more than 150 years. In 1781 an Italian doctor living in England experimented with a cooling process based on the principle of evaporation and the compression of air. Further experiments were undertaken in the early nineteenth century in America and England, and in 1824 a British patent was granted on the use of sulphuric acid in an absorption process, by which quantities of ice were made in demonstrations. In 1834 Jacob Perkins of Massachusetts patented a steam-driven machine to make ice. This was further developed by Dr Gorrie of Florida, who in 1851 patented an ice-making machine. Similar machines were developed at the end of the century, but they were large and cumbersome and were only used commercially. Household refrigerators were proposed as early as 1887 and a number were on the market by 1895. The working parts of refrigerators were built separately and often installed in the purchaser's own ice-cooled cabinet. Sometimes the components were put outside the cabinet, but The Guardian refrigerator of 1915 had a self-contained freezing unit. The cabinet was made of solid oak, with seaweed for insulation. It contained 2 ice trays, 5 wire shelves and had a capacity of 9 cubic feet. Contemporary cookery books show that this new method of cooling food produced a spate of ice-chilled recipes, many of which were often quite unsuitable.

Lord Braye, who lived at Stanford Hall, Rugby, was extremely proud of his first automatic refrigerator, which he purchased in the 1920s. The household had previously used an ice house and a wooden ice chest filled with home-produced ice, although electricity had been installed in the 1890s. He led his dinner guests down to the basement to admire the new machine, but found that Cook was not yet adjusted to the new ways and the refrigerator contained only a small piece of cheese and a pair of shoes.

Early ice cream had to be packed into moulds and frozen in ice caves or chests, but a better texture was obtained by churning or beating the ice cream. It is said that American Nancy Johnson invented the first ice-cream freezer in 1864. The earliest ice-cream makers were constructed in wood and consisted of an open-topped box containing a second box, which could be cranked by a handle on the butter-churn principle. A later development was a wooden pail containing a metal cylinder, and incorporating a paddle, which was worked by a handle. The simple Star ice-cream freezer was made of white wood with a tin cylinder; the Paragon was a superior model made of oak with a pewter cylinder. The Glaciator was a smaller flatter tub with a wide sweeping paddle fitted to a crank handle. The freezing agent was originally a mixture of ice and salt, but by 1890 'Inexhaustible Freezing Crystals' could be purchased by the tin. An unusual variation on the ice-cream maker was the American Freezer, marketed in England by Harrods. This was a cylinder mounted on a cast-iron stand. The freezer did not

Elaborate wooden icebox with porcelain and metal fittings; American, 1880

Shepard's Lightning ice-cream machine, *c.* 1900, imported from the USA for sale in England. A double gear operated by the handle turns both the drum within the wooden pail (which is packed with ice and freezing salt) and the mixing paddles inside the drum. The illustrations of moulds are in Mrs A. B. Marshall's *Book of Ices* of the same period.

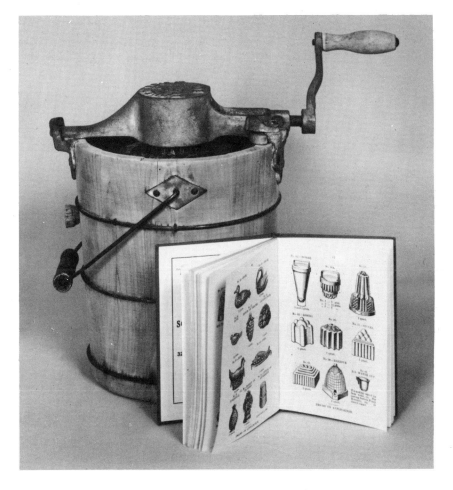

involve churning, but could freeze one or two ice-cream moulds and also took a bottle of wine.

The Spong ice-cream freezer was a metal cylinder mounted horizontally on a stand with the handle fitted like that on a manual sewing machine. This was advertised for family use and for restaurants and confectioners, and could produce 'ice-cream or solid bars of ice on an average of every five minutes until the ice and salt have dissolved'. It could also be used to prepare freezing salts which could then be packed into the more traditional ice-cream freezer.

7 Moulds, Cutters and Serving Equipment

English wooden gingerbread mould decorated with a pair of lovebirds

Opposite A variety of copper pans including a fish kettle in the kitchen at Hardwick Hall, Derbyshire. The illustration clearly shows how the dresser evolved from an arrangement of shelves fitted above the old side table used for 'dressing' food.

It was always a matter of pride to present sweet dishes attractively. The housewife was offered a range of fanciful cutters and moulds to help her, and these were usually based on the traditional country motifs of flowers, animals and birds.

Gingerbread was tremendously popular, given as gifts and sold at fairs, and it was often gilded and formed into fancy shapes. From the time of Henry VII onwards the gingerbread was heavily embossed by means of patterned rolling pins. It is thought that gingerbread moulds came to England from Italy in Elizabeth I's reign, and they were made in boxwood, beech, walnut and pear wood. Moulds might be square, round or heart-shaped, and varied from primitive designs to very elaborate ones, which were probably used for cakes of marzipan, pressed into the mould while warm.

English moulds tended to be less elaborate than those used in Europe and America. Patterns of birds and flowers were popular, but some moulds were decorated with sporting scenes, initials, or elaborate coats of arms. Commercial bakers used double-sided moulds which featured a decorative pattern on one side, and the name of the maker and his town on the other. In Scotland the shortbread thistle mould is still in use today.

Tin cutters were popular for other types of biscuit and cookie. The heart was a popular motif, together with the two-headed bird, the cockerel, the pig, and a woman wearing a long dress. A number of individual cutters were sometimes included in one large circle. A simple round cutter equipped with spikes was known as a pricker and docker; longer spikes indicated an implement which could only prick but not cut.

Sets of cutters were popular in the late nineteenth century. The tiny cutters used for *petits fours* were known as brilliant cutters and were packed a dozen to a tin. A variety of fancy cutters might be packed into a wide flat tin, and concentric fluted circular cutters were sometimes arranged in a tin in a rose pattern. Particularly popular were the sets of twelve tear-shaped cutters, ranging in size and packed one inside the other. With a plain or fluted edge, these were known as cutlet patterns.

Before cottages had ovens, it was common practice to take bread and pies to be baked in a community village oven. The loaves had to be

84

Tin cookie cutter; American,
19th century

Right Hinged metal mould for baking
raised game pies; English, 19th
century

Left The old kitchen in the Shirley
Plantation, Virginia, with two fine
tables, a collection of copper moulds,
and a small Windsor chair

stamped with the owner's initials and a special marker was sometimes used. This was an oblong plate about 3 inches long made of iron plated with tin. On the upper side was the handle and on the base were inch-high letters about $\frac{1}{2}$ inch deep.

Piecrusts or 'coffins' were traditionally made from a pastry of hot water, fat and flour and contained a filling of meat, game or fruit. The paste was very soft and malleable, and was shaped with the hands round a pie mould, sometimes known as a 'wood'. This was a simple cylinder made of wood with a short handle at the top. The mould was removed from the pastry case, which was filled and lidded before baking. A more sophisticated type of mould had a metal bottom with fluted edges, and this was pressed down to shape and decorate the lid.

Game pies needed a more elaborate finish than those made with such cottage food as pork or gooseberries. A hinged pie tin, oval in shape and with a decorative embossed pattern on the inside, was used for game pies. The pastry was baked inside the mould, which could be easily removed towards the finish of baking to brown the pastry.

In upper-class households the pastry case of a game pie was not usually eaten but was given to the servants or animals. In the nineteenth century the pastry was often dispensed with altogether, and recipes specified that the filling should be baked in an oval or round dish. This was usually coloured and shaped like pastry, with a decorative lid which often features a model of a game bird or animal, or a group of wild creatures.

A mixture of chopped meat and meat jelly known as brawn was very popular, and was the recognized way of using animal heads, tongues

Left Lidded hot-water jug (1800); 18th-century brass flour dredger; wooden gingerbread mould; and wooden sugar mould (1870) used for making cake decorations

Below Set of individual copper moulds on a turned wooden stand; English, 19th century. This type of mould was used for a variety of sweet and savoury creams and jellies.

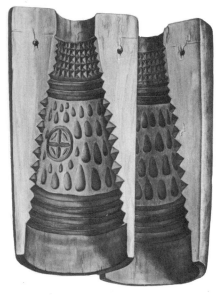

Early 19th-century decorated pine mould from Connecticut for making a cone of maple sugar. The two halves of the mould were held together by iron bands.

and spare rabbits or chickens. Brawn moulds were usually cylindrical in shape like a saucepan, with a lid and a metal disc which could be weighted down to compress the contents. The Improved Brawn Mould of 1895 featured an adjustable screw, which was fitted to the disc. The gadget could also be used to press and shape ox tongues.

Another type of specialized mould is the American maple sugar mould, a decorative wooden double-sided mould, which was used to form a conical loaf from the liquid sugar. Ordinary refined sugar was also moulded into cones or 'sugar loaves', but these moulds were undecorated.

All kinds of puddings, ice cream and butter were shaped in highly decorative moulds made of copper, tin, pewter, glass or earthenware. Hinged pewter moulds were used for ice cream and also butter, which could be chilled in the ice cave. These had detachable lids and bases so that the contents could be unmoulded straight on to the plate. They were often designed to resemble vegetables or fruit, and the pineapple (a symbol of welcome) was a favourite motif. Richer families could afford copper moulds for jellies and creams, and also for savoury jellies. These were often made in elaborate castle shapes, but others were designed as border or ring moulds, which were used for savoury timbales and for shaping circles of rice. Copper entrée moulds had such fancy names as The Crawfish, King Fisher, Hare, Fancy Cutlet, Cutlet, Sandwich, Ham, Bird's Nest, Ox Tongue, and Chicken.

Less elaborate tin moulds were used for sweet jellies, for making moulds of vegetables and other savoury dishes, and for baking cakes. Those with a fitted lid could also be used for steaming puddings. Moulds specifically designed for cakes sometimes had small supporting feet as it was difficult to rest the mould on its curved and patterned base. The Pennyslvania Dutch were particularly fond of a simple melon-shaped mould.

Brown saltglaze moulds with a decorative pattern on the base were popular for cottage use. So too were heavy earthenware moulds which copied the shapes of the more expensive copper moulds. Wedgwood produced a wide range of creamware moulds in simple oval, round or lozenge shapes, with beautifully modelled designs on the base. These designs varied from classical themes featuring cherubs and animals to horses, goats, sheep, lions, sitting hens, dogs, bunches of grapes and groups of game birds. Animals were popular designs for jellies, perhaps for the nursery table, and occasionally an earthenware mould is found in the shape of a duck or rabbit on a raised base.

A curious type of china jelly mould, often not recognized, was supplied with a separate wedge-shaped piece of china. This fitted inside the mould, and when the jelly was turned out the embedded wedge of china acted as a support. It is very rare to find a mould complete with wedge, but the prettily painted wedges can be found alone.

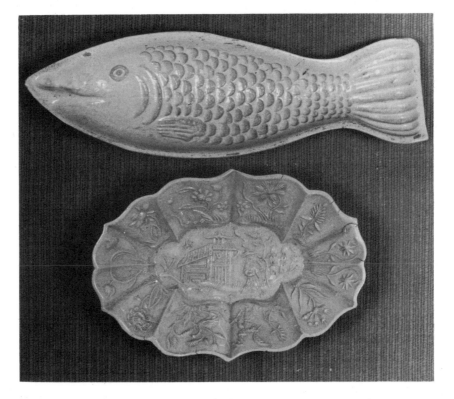

Right Staffordshire salt-glazed stoneware mould in the shape of a fish, and a fluted meat tray, 1745

Below Pierced mould for making Italian cream, blancmange mould specially produced by Brown & Polson, makers of cornflour (corn-starch), and a stoneware jelly mould with a flower design; English, 19th century

Right American wooden shortbread mould. The design of the kilted figure, with rose and thistle emblems, combined with wheatsheaves, suggests that this mould may have been taken to America by an early settler from Scotland.

Below Heavy pewter moulds used to shape ice cream or butter. The detachable lids and bases allowed the contents to be removed easily without spoiling the pattern. This set was originally used at Magdalene College, Cambridge.

Oval china stands with pierced holes were made to match meat, vegetable and fish serving dishes, and were designed so that meat juices or surplus liquid should drain through to the base of the dish. Although they were actually used in the dining room, drainers were kept in the kitchen. The stands display a wide range of china patterns, but are rarely found complete with their dishes.

Decorative egg stands were originally kept in the kitchen, but later were used in the dining room. They were left on the sideboard so that each person could boil his own eggs for breakfast when needed. An early Staffordshire slipware egg stand of 1690 has six holes for the eggs, but later designs sometimes incorporated simple egg cups which slotted into the holes. Occasionally made in wood, these stands were more often rather pretty pieces of cottage china, made in fanciful curlicued square or circles, with a loop handle, and decorated with gilding or painted flowers.

8 Labour-Saving Devices

Although many households employed a number of servants to help in the kitchen, labour-saving gadgets were popular for dealing with routine jobs. Special implements were developed for chopping and pounding, grating, shredding, squeezing and mixing, and these retained the same simple shapes for centuries. In the late eighteenth century essential items became more decorative, but it was not until the mid-nineteenth century that the more elaborate or mechanical type of device appeared as the shortage of servants began to make itself felt.

Pastry and biscuits were usually rolled out on a smooth flat board. Made of both hard and soft woods, these boards are usually oblong or round, with a pierced handle for hanging on the wall. In America these boards were used to roll out the paste for making noodles. In the Midlands, North of England and Scotland, oatcakes were rolled out on a haverboard, also known as a riddleboard or bakbrede. The boards were carved with criss-cross lines, and the flat oatcakes retained the pattern after baking.

Pastry crimpers were used for trimming and marking pie crusts. These little tools are also known as pastry wheels, jiggers, dough trimmers and dough wheels, and may be found in a variety of patterns. The simplest type of crimper has a wheel at one end attached to a short handle. An elaborate American version made of wrought iron has a long curved handle in the shape of a bird. At the beginning of the nineteenth century a manufacturer of Birmingham, England, advertised small implements described as paste jiggers and tweezers, made in brass or iron. These pastry decorators incorporated flexible grooved or crimped tweezers instead of a handle.

The same Birmingham manufacturer also advertised steel and brass larding pins. These metal pins ranged from 6 to 10 inches in length, and had a hollowed out tube split into four at one end, and a sharp point at the other. Pieces of fat or bacon were placed in the open end, and the pin was then used in the same way as a needle and thread to insert the strips of fat into a joint of meat before roasting.

The preparation of fruit inspired some of the earliest and most primitive gadgets, and also some of the most intricate machines. The earliest implements for coring fruit were apple scoops, made from the metacarpal bones of sheep, hollowed out and roughly ornamented with criss-cross hatchings. These were often used to scoop all the flesh from

Mechanical food chopper, which could also be used for mixing; English, late 19th century

Right Jagging wheel in the shape of a sea serpent made from whalebone, and a combined pastry cutter, grater and can opener made from wood and tin; American, 19th century

the apple, leaving the skin intact, and were useful for those who had lost their teeth. A primitive American corer consisted of an iron hook at the end of a smoothly rounded handle. Later examples were made of bone and mounted on wooden handles, which were inlaid with brass and sometimes engraved with the name of the owner. Other varieties were made from carved ivory and from wood.

The earliest machines for peeling and coring apples were probably made in America. A cast-iron apple parer patented in 1873 by Messrs Landers, Frary & Clark of Boston, Mass., was a development of the interlocking-wheel machine. This was a complicated arrangement of cog wheels and blade, and was mounted on a stand which could be clamped to the table.

Two other gadgets were perfected for simple fruit-preparation jobs. A raisin stoner patented in England in 1898 resembled a miniature mincing machine. The raisins were first washed and were fed into the machine while still wet; a serrated roller extracted the pips and disgorged the squashed raisins from a small chute. The American cast-iron cherry pipper of 1860 had a feeder and chute, and was mounted on a stand; when a handle was turned it drove a rod, which extracted the cherry stones.

The Universal marmalade cutter, made in England in 1900, was another heavy iron machine to clamp to a table. Fruit was fed through a hopper and pushed down with a wooden pestle. The oranges were chopped by a blade attached to a heavy lever, which could be worked to and fro. Like so many of these gadgets, the cutter produced somewhat bruised and crushed fruit.

All kinds of foods were chopped with heavy iron blades, cast in one piece with iron handles, or mounted on wooden handles. Some

96

Three mechanical devices for preparing fruit: *left* The Universal Marmalade chopper, English, early 20th century; *right* patent raisin stoner, English, 1898; *below* cast-iron cherry pipper, American, 1863

Three 19th-century vegetable or herb choppers with different types of blades and turned handles. In the centre is a scraper for removing dough from the trough; at the top is a bread rasp used for scraping the tops of over-baked loaves, and for grating stale bread to make breadcrumbs.

choppers had curved blades, which could be used in round bowls or kitchen mortars; others had straight-edged blades and were used with chopping boards. Another type of chopper, requiring the use of both hands, was made up of three parallel iron blades, which curve upwards and are finished with two knob handles. An unusual eighteenth-century American herb chopper consisted of a cast-iron wheel pierced by a double-ended wooden handle. The herbs were finely chopped by rolling the wheel up and down a boat-shaped iron bowl mounted on legs. Mechanical food choppers were in use by the late nineteenth century, and were employed for cutting up suet and vegetables. The food was placed in a metal container mounted on a wooden stand; when a handle was turned the metal drum revolved and a chopping blade, attached to a levered arm, rose and fell.

98

Right Double-bladed iron food-
chopper with twin handles

Above Pennsylvania Dutch carved
wooden cabbage slicer, 19th century.
This was an essential implement for
the preparation of sauerkraut for
winter storage.

Right Pennsylvania Dutch food-
chopper in the shape of a fox,
mid-19th century

Special cutters were essential wherever cabbage was regularly
made into sauerkraut. The Pennsylvania Dutch used wooden cutters
fitted with single or multiple forged blades. These ranged in size from
small hand utensils for everyday use, to larger cutters fitted over casks,
which could hold three or four grated cabbages at a time. These
oblong-shaped cabbage cutters were usually made in walnut, with
decorative pierced handles, and they were often painted with gaily
coloured motifs.

In addition to chopping utensils there was a wide range of graters
and rasps for use in the kitchen. The bread rasp, a rough-surfaced
blade of iron mounted on a handle, was used for scraping the bottom of
burned loaves, and also for grating dry bread to make crumbs. The
dough scraper was a similar implement, but was used for scraping
surplus dough from the sides of a kneading trough.

Tin graters were widely used for dealing with bread, cheese and

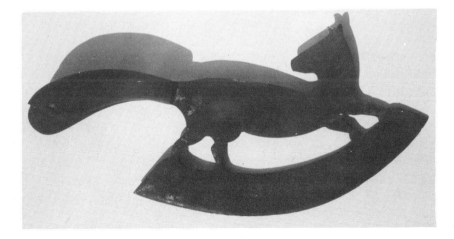

A wooden and tin grating box with a drawer beneath to catch the grated food

spices, and may be found in a variety of forms. Large graters were sometimes cylindrical in shape, or curved with a flat back and a simple metal handle. A number of examples consisted of a flat grating surface fitted over a box to catch the grated food. Single-sided graters were sometimes mounted on small feet, and were fitted with a wooden spool handle. Another useful type was the small oval pierced tin grater with a curved hoop-shaped handle; this was rubbed over a stale loaf to make breadcrumbs.

Spices were supplied whole and had to be ground at home. Spice graters were often very small, and were sometimes incorporated in spice boxes. Tiny decorative wooden graters attached to small boxes were not for kitchen use; they were carried on the person so that nutmeg could be grated into hot drinks and punches.

Lemon squeezers were almost always made of wood, since metal was quickly discoloured by the juice. A simple type of small hand squeezer had a short handle and a bulbous end which curved to a point, and which was carved with deep twisted grooves. A larger type of lemon squeezer consisted of a thick board mounted on four short legs. The lemon half was placed in a hollow in the board, and the juice was squeezed out when the domed lid was pressed down on top of the lemon.

White sugar was made in a cone about 36 inches high, and weighing about 14 lb. Large households bought whole cones wrapped in blue paper and stored them in a cradle of string, suspended from hooks in the ceiling. Smaller households would buy from the grocer pieces broken off the sugar loaf. The sugar had to be cut into small pieces for

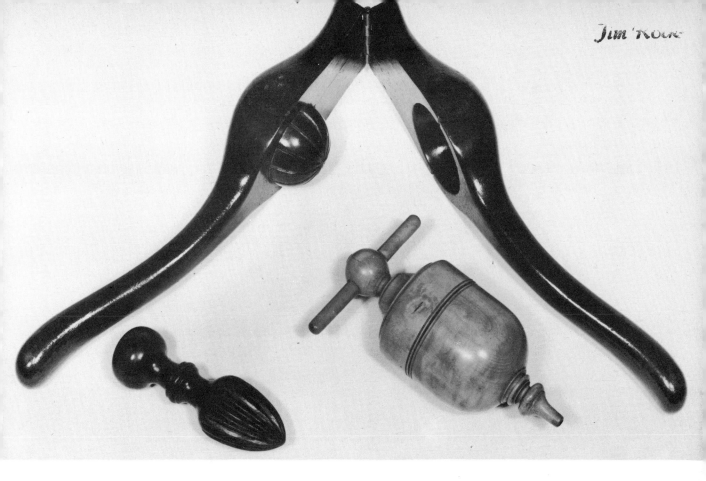

Three varieties of wooden lemon
squeezers in use in English kitchens in
the 18th and 19th centuries

table use, and the lumps were then powdered with a pestle and mortar
and sometimes sieved for cooking purposes. Sugar nippers resemble
a large pair of tongs or scissors, with outward curving blades ending in
sharp pincers. They often have elaborately incised decorations on the
boss joining the cutter arms, and a short metal support to stand them
on the table. Sugar nippers were available in a variety of sizes, and it is
possible that the smaller hand models were most frequently used at
table. Heavier iron nippers were mounted on wooden blocks and were
more suitable for kitchen use to break up the larger pieces of sugar.
The heavy cast-iron nippers made by Bartlett & Son of Bristol were
almost certainly for use in shops. They consisted of two curved pieces of
metal which could enclose the whole cone of sugar.

Pestles and mortars were important pieces of equipment, and most
kitchens possessed more than one set. The bowls were often used for
mixing, but they were also used in combination with a pestle to crush
spices, nuts and any other food which had to be reduced to a fine
consistency. Mortars came in a variety of sizes and materials. Stoneware, wood and metal were commonly used, and many were elaborately
turned or painted. The accompanying pestle was sometimes made of
turned wood, metal, or of marble with a turned wooden handle.
Spice was usually ground in a metal mortar with a metal pestle, as
this was easy to keep dry; these metal utensils were also used for
preparing medicinal remedies at home.

Opposite A fine dresser with guard rail, storage cupboards and drawers, complete with pottery made in Pennsylvania between 1765–1830, from the Kershner Parlor at the Winterthur Museum

Heavy iron sugar cutters mounted on wood and used for breaking up sugar loaves; American, late 18th century. This type of cutter was most commonly used in the kitchen, while more delicately made nippers without stands were for table use.

In the mid-nineteenth century ground coffee could be bought from the grocer, who would probably own a large cast-iron mill. At the same time, smaller coffee grinders for use in the home became fashionable. These comprised a pine or walnut box, surmounted by a metal grinder with a long handle, and incorporating a drawer for the ground coffee. Sometimes the grinder consisted of a pewter or cast-iron bowl into which the coffee beans were placed. Other models, often elaborately decorated, had a covered grinding area with a sliding lid.

Mincers and grinders were used for making sausages, since it was not easy to cut the meat finely enough by hand. Meat cutters such as the Perfection, or the varieties made by Messrs Spong, could be clamped to the table, and are similar to models still made today. Sometimes mincers were supplied with a pierced cone, which could be attached to the machine to feed the minced meat into the sausage skins. A very early English sausage machine of a different design consisted of a box of maple lined with pewter. Inside were two rows of eight teeth arranged in a spiral to push the meat against sharp steel blades for mincing.

Dough was commonly kneaded by hand, while eggs and cake mixtures were beaten with the bare hands, or with a wooden spoon, a fork or a bent wire whisk. The Holt Egg Beater of 1899 was a

Left The kitchen at Clandon Park, Surrey, showing a variety of spits and copper utensils, and a fine Windsor chair

Below left The kitchen at Cotehele House, showing a rack for storing bacon, cauldrons suspended over the open fire, and a wooden salt box on the wall

Right Grimwade's 'Quick Cooker' bowl, patented 1909, for preparing the steamed puddings so popular at the turn of the century

This 19th-century digester was the forerunner of today's pressure cooker. A conical weight was fitted inside, and the lid was raised to allow steam to escape when pressure exceeded 2–3 lb.

mechanical hand whisk which speeded up the process of beating. A more elaborate device was the food chopper already described, which could also be used for mixing. A slightly different action was incorporated in the Universal Bread Maker patented in 1900. This was a tin bucket with paddles fitted inside; when a handle was turned the paddles revolved to knead the dough into a ball.

During the nineteenth century there were a number of devices which utilized steam pressure to speed up cooking, and to economize on fuel. In America Mrs Henry Ward Beecher used a Hill Champion Odorless Steam Cooker, and testified that it was 'destined to make home duties much less oppressive. It will also prepare food more properly, and in less time, than any contrivance I have yet seen'. Her model consisted of a large two-tier steamer, fitted with a lock cover and water-joint, a tube to carry away smells and surplus steam, and an adjustable partition. A selection of vegetables, a casserole dish and a pudding could all be cooked together on a range, oil or gas stove. The quick-cooker bowl was a simple little device, which was patented by Grimwade at the beginning of the twentieth century. This had a fitting lid which formed a watertight seal, and did away with the old-fashioned pudding cloth. The bowls were supposed to cook the contents quickly from the centre outwards, and could also be used for keeping food hot.

The forerunner of the modern pressure cooker was the digester, used in the nineteenth century for softening bones to make soup or broth. This was a heavy cast-iron saucepan with a looped handle. The

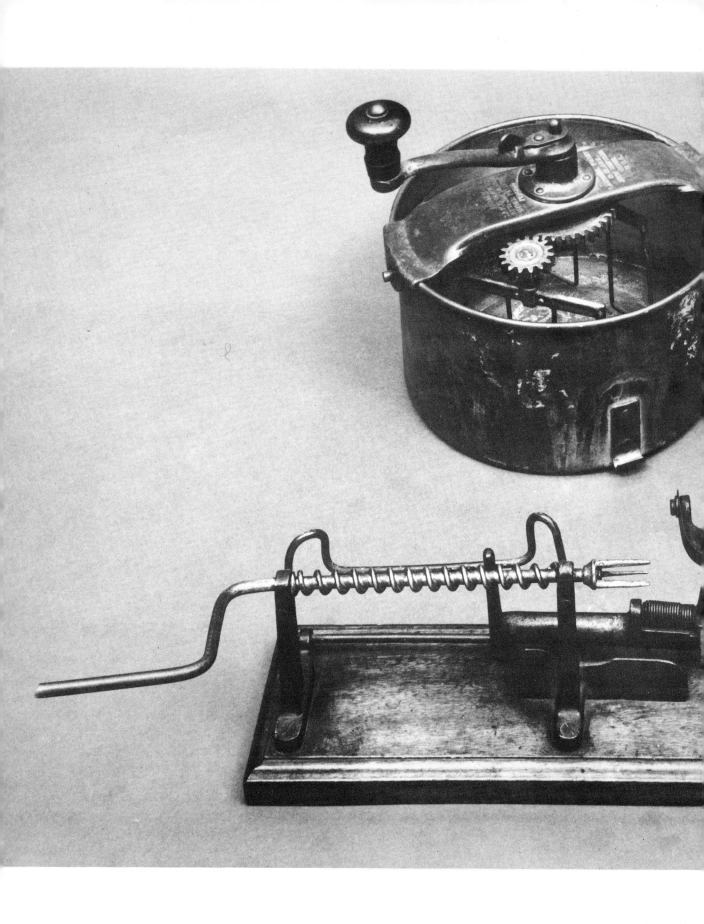

lid was fitted with a valve which could be raised to allow steam to escape when pressure exceeded 2 or 3 lb.

Electricity was not widely used for kitchen equipment until just before 1914. An early electric toaster made in America by the General Electric Company had four vertical elements mounted on a porcelain base, with a heavy wire rack on each side to hold the bread. It was necessary to turn the bread by hand to toast both sides. The first automatic toaster appeared in 1918, but even by 1921 the rate of production was only one toaster a day. Other electric luxuries produced about 1911 by the Westinghouse Electric Corporation in America included an electric toaster oven and an electric frying pan, while the Angelus Campfire Company of Chicago produced the Bar-B-Q Marshmallow Toaster.

Below A plug-in electric frying pan made by Westinghouse of America in 1911. The design of the pan with its legged stand makes it look very like the medieval skillet which stood in the open hearth.

Left Patent cake mixer, 1896, and a complicated device for peeling potatoes, *c.* 1870

9 Convenience Foods and Cleaning Materials

THE MOST COMPLETE CHOCOLATE PLANT
IN THE UNITED STATES.

HERSHEY'S
STERILIZED
MILK
CHOCOLATE

MADE FROM THE
BEST CHOCOLATE AND PURE,
RICH MILK AND SUGAR.

HERSHEY CHOCOLATE CO.
LANCASTER, PA. U.S.A.

Above Wrappers and advertisements for chocolate confectionery stressed purity and health, but the curly-headed child emerging from a cocoa bean probably had more sales appeal.

Left By the middle of the 19th century American manufacturers were producing a wide range of jams, jellies and preserves formerly prepared by the mistress of the house and her servants. This advertisement shows wooden tubs, jelly glasses and preserving jars, which are similar to the traditional containers used in the home kitchen.

Until about 1830 the housewife was expected to do a great deal more than simply keep the house clean and prepare food for the family and servants. She also had to be the family doctor and beautician, preparing preventive and curative medicines and a variety of beauty preparations. She preserved all her own food, made sauces, pickles and jams, and devised delicious sweetmeats. Even the basic cooking and cleaning were not simple operations, for seeds and spices had to be ground, setting agents prepared from animal bones, raising agents prepared from ale, polishes and washing materials made from beeswax, sieved ashes and other home-produced ingredients.

Chocolate was perhaps the first of the manufactured foods to appear on the market, with a plant erected in England in 1728, another in Germany in 1756, France in 1760 and America in 1765. But even this process of manufacture only released the chocolate centres of the cocoa beans, which had to be crushed and heated before mixing with milk.

Millers and innkeepers were the first to use their talents to produce aids for the housewife. The millers were able to make use of their adaptable machinery, while the innkeepers often had enterprising wives who made their names with individual sauces and pickles. Increasing travel, particularly to the East, inspired many new recipes for sauces, curry powders and relishes, and the housewife, faced with a shortage of kitchen staff and a lack of time and inclination for tedious jobs, began to appreciate the first convenience foods.

Food firms grew through the enterprise of far-sighted men. Harvey's Sauce, an essential of Victorian cookery, was first produced at the end of the eighteenth century by one Elizabeth Harvey, sister of a Middlesex innkeeper. She married a London grocer called Lazenby, and made a fortune for her husband by putting on the market a wide variety of convenience foods, including Lazenby's Essence of Anchovies, another popular nineteenth-century seasoning. From this small beginning there grew up a firm renowned for the high quality of its bottled and canned goods. Worcestershire Sauce had a similarly romantic story, with the original recipe brought back from India in the 1830s by Lord Sandys, a Governor of the State of Bengal. The recipe was made up for him by two chemists, Mr John Lea and Mr William Perrins of Worcester, England, and the reputation of the sauce made their fortunes and founded a world-wide industry.

Early 20th-century convenience foods emphasized purity and speed of preparation. Jell-O's appeal was 'delicate, delightful, dainty'.

While housewives had little difficulty in accepting flavouring aids, they were not so sure of the real labour-savers. As with kitchen equipment, the men who had advanced ideas saw them rejected, and new products often did not achieve success for fifty or a hundred years after they had been invented. Refined flour, to help the housewife to make lighter cakes, first appeared on the American market in 1856. Swans Down Family Flour was first advertised in 1876, and in 1894 the Ingleheart brothers pioneered the first packaged cake mix. This was known as Instant Swans Down, to which only milk had to be added. The result was a dismal failure. The brothers continued to work on their cake flour, receiving a grand prize at the World's Fair in St Louis in 1904, and in 1926 they joined General Foods. However, it was not until 1948

An advertisement of 1915 for Campbell's Soup combines child appeal and humour, two qualities which were considered important sales points by pioneer advertisers

that cake mixes really became a commercial success. It was said that women needed to 'add an egg' to feel that they were doing any work, for a household task that was too easy produced a sense of guilt.

Often the food we take for granted today was the result of a chance happening or an unlikely partnership. America's famous Baker's Coconut was the result of a Philadelphia flour miller accepting a load of coconuts from war-ridden Cuba in payment for a shipment of flour in 1895. Mr Baker was swamped with a commodity which was then considered to be a rarity. He loaded the coconuts on to a goods train and telegraphed the grocery buyers along the line to come to their stations to buy coconuts at special prices. Having been unable to sell the whole shipment, he devised a method of preparing the nut meats and sold them to local confectioners and pastry cooks. The new flavour was very popular with housewives and Franklin Baker subsequently became known as the Coconut King.

Campbell's soups were the result of a partnership in 1869 between Joseph Campbell, a fruit merchant, and Abram Anderson, an ice-box manufacturer. Together they decided to can tomatoes, vegetables, jellies, seasonings and mincemeat, all of which items were formerly produced in the home. They entered the soup market as early as 1897, when they were joined by one Dr Dorrance, who originated canned condensed soup.

Food products stimulated the use of advertising and inspired new promotional methods. The first American patent for a gelatine dessert was taken out in 1845 by Peter Cooper, but it was not until 1895 that Pearl B. Wait, a cough medicine manufacturer of New York, decided to enter the new packaged food business. He adapted Cooper's idea, coined the name Jell-O, and started production in 1897. In spite of the new-style trade name, there were few sales, and the company was sold to another manufacturer, Francis Woodward. He too had a slow start with the product, but began an advertising campaign in 1902. The advertisements showed women with wavy curls and fashionable buns dressed in white aprons and wearing triumphant smiles, proclaiming that Jell-O Gelatin was 'America's Most Famous Dessert'. A picture of the Jell-O Girl appeared on each package, and this was soon followed by magazine advertisements and store displays. Later there were sponsored recipe booklets, gelatine moulds, special spoons and serving dishes, and delivery vans painted with the firm's name and slogan. Altogether this was a big step forward from the early nineteenth-century handbills and mid-century classified newspaper advertisements, which were the traditional means of advertising to the household.

Colman's of Norwich, manufacturers of convenience foods and laundry aids, were a firm who recognized the full value of advertising. Although powdered mustard had been introduced by a Mrs Clements of Durham in 1720, it was not until 1742 that the condiment was commercially produced by Keens of London. Jeremiah Colman started

Right Laundry aids produced by J. & J. Colman were first made in 1832, and included many varieties of starch and laundry blue. At the turn of the century starch was packed in cardboard boxes with pictorial labels (centre and centre-right of picture), illustrating nursery rhymes or life in foreign lands. Mustard was also used for medicinal purposes, and bath mustard (right foreground) was a popular turn-of-the-century product.

to mill mustard in 1814, and founded his huge commercial empire, which eventually took in Keens and many other small firms. They specialized in starch and laundry blue, and cereal products. It is interesting to note that at the beginning of the nineteenth century there were severe restrictive practices on the manufacture of starch. A licence was needed, a tenement rent was exacted, the manufacturing process was regulated, and 75 per cent. of the market value was levied in tax.

In America it was expected that trade marks would be 'appropriate and graceful'; in England customer acceptance depended on 'a tasteful style'. Accordingly, such firms as Colman's commissioned famous artists to produce posters and label designs, which often relied heavily on child appeal. They devised slogans which would sell subtly and become household words, without giving offence. For all manufacturers it was important to stress high quality, and it was common practice to include a 'certificate of authenticity' on packaging. This carried the manufacturer's signature and often a money-back guarantee if the product did not reach the advertised standard of 'purity'—a key word in early convenience-food manufacture. Testimonials from the principals of cookery schools, from aristocrats and even (for Borwick's baking powder) from the Queen's baker were considered an important part of advertising.

Early advertising material is scarce, since it was easily destroyed. At the beginning of the nineteenth century handbills were used to advertise wares, and included details of the food or preparation, a list of stockists, sometimes a recipe, testimonials from satisfied users, and a certificate of authenticity. With the growth of literacy, advertising was transferred to newspapers, women's magazines, and household or cookery books.

Posters, showcards and enamel signs became increasingly popular as people began to travel more. Famous artists were employed to design posters, and many of the results were highly decorative but uninformative. It was thought that people enjoyed seeing a colourful and attractive picture, even if it failed to tell them anything about the product, although on the whole it was only the old-established and well-known firms who could afford to risk this type of advertising. Colman's advertisements for laundry blue, for instance, included pictures of a town crier (possibly by Sir Alfred Munnings), a ploughman by Cecil Aldin, two small boys in sailor suits, and an oarsman in a rowing boat. Sometimes there was an attempt at heavy-handed humour, such as the picture of a greyhound racing along with a stiff collar in its mouth to advertise starch, or the butterfly with the slogan 'Everybody is attracted by Colman's Blue'. Showcards for counter and window display were generally more informative, and enamel signs were almost stark by comparison, usually featuring only the name of the product or a brief slogan in eye-catching colours. Companies employed outdoor staff for the sole purpose of fixing advertising signs to every available wall.

Left Early 20th-century convenience foods marketed by J. & J. Colman Ltd. The square mustard tin and the jar of prepared mustard are of the type taken to the Antartic by Captain Scott in 1907. The commemorative tin, one of a series produced yearly from 1880 to 1939, marked the occasion of the coronation of Edward VII. The patent barley and oats, acquired from Keen Robinson & Co by J. & J. Colman in 1903, had first won acclaim when used by the royal households of William IV and Queen Victoria.

Apple butter, a traditional American preserve, was manufactured by Heinz and packed in home-style containers.

Containers for food and cleaning materials are more easily found. Like the posters, they were designed to catch the eye with their complicated designs beautifully printed in many colours. Elaborate trademarks, fruit and flowers, children and cherubs, and pictures of factories were the most popular themes for the wrappers of sweets and chocolates, early canned goods, bottles and box labels. Many of these designs were in fact prepared for collectors. Colman's labels for their starch boxes were designed in series of nursery or patriotic pictures especially for Victorian scrapbooks. Printed tins became very popular, particularly for presentation purposes. Even mustard was put into specially large and elaborate Christmas tins, while biscuits and sweets (in earlier years made at home or purchased loose) appeared in tins which were made in a variety of fanciful shapes, such as a row of books, a pile of plates or even a handbag.

Early glass and china containers closely resembled those in which the housewife had traditionally preserved her own produce. Heinz packed their apple butter in stone jars and wooden tubs, and their early 'catsup' in elaborate glass jars. Scottish marmalade manufacturers chose to pack their preserve in stone jars, while the American firm of Gordon & Dilworth, established in 1847, preferred traditional wooden tubs, and prettily shaped jelly glasses for their more delicate jams. Elizabeth Young started selling fish at Greenwich in 1805 and the family concern later developed into a large-scale business. When they entered the prepared food industry at the beginning of the twentieth century, they used the traditional shallow earthenware pot in which fish and meat had been preserved in butter or 'potted' since Elizabethan times. This type of pot was used until 1939, when it was superseded first by cheaper and more practical wax board, and in later years by plastic, but still based on the original pot design.

A tremendous variety of promotional material was devised by manufacturers to advertise their goods. Diaries, almanacs and calendars were traditional Christmas gifts to the kitchen from the retailer to ensure custom in the following year, but the manufacturers also found it convenient to keep their name to the fore by personalizing many everyday objects. Utensils for specific products, such as Oxo and Bovril mugs, Jell-O moulds and spoons, Brown & Polson blancmange moulds and Colman's mustard pots, were all very popular. These were not trashy novelties, but souvenirs to be treasured. The mustard pots, for instance, were made by such famous firms as Copeland, Doulton, Lambeth, Stourbridge and Minton. Other favourite giveaways were books for children, handkerchiefs, tape measures, spy glasses, tobacco tins, pencil sharpeners, paperweights, bookmarks and match holders, all in constant use and serving as a reminder of a favourite brand. Miniature packs were also produced, and were particularly popular with children.

A traditional English delicacy, Yarmouth Bloater Paste. This type of commercial food was available as early as the second half of the 18th century.

The "ORIGINAL"
BRAND'S

BLOATER PASTE.

H. W. BRAND (Limited.
6, Vere St., Oxford St., W.

COLMAN'S
MUSTAR
Colman's
Mustard
Little Naturalist
ILLUSTRATED BY JOHN HASSALL
BLUE
BEARD
A
Mustard Club
Menu

Left A group of promotional items issued by Colman's, including mustard pots by Minton (1902), Doulton of Lambeth (1884), Copeland and Doulton (1900). Other promotional items issued between 1900 and 1910 include a wooden clothes peg, tape measure, pencil sharpener in the form of a tiny mustard tin, tobacco tin, magnifying glass, string dispensing tin, match holder, feeding bowl and children's books.

A variety of moulds for creams and jellies, including early advertising gifts from Jell-O

Many of the new products required special cooking techniques and women had to be taught how to use them. To maintain sales, women also had to be encouraged to use a product in a dozen different ways, so the manufacturers produced recipe leaflets and booklets. In England Chivers' jelly packets contained coloured cards depicting a variety of fancy puddings, but in America Jell-O launched into full-scale booklets, which were distributed door-to-door throughout the country. These were available in many languages, including Yiddish, and were illustrated with brightly coloured pictures. The favourite recipes of well-known people, such as actress Ethel Barrymore, were reproduced, and work was done by famous illustrators, including Rose Cecil O'Neill, who created the Kewpies to advertise the product. In some years, as many as 15 million booklets were printed.

The personal testimonial was always important in advertising recipe booklets. Borwick's Baking Powder, advertised in their own book quite

Right An early 20th-century large-scale display packet of cornflour (cornstarch) with facsimile signatures of manufactures, Brown & Polson

Below Paper labels for early canned convenience foods stress the homely quality of dishes formerly prepared in every kitchen

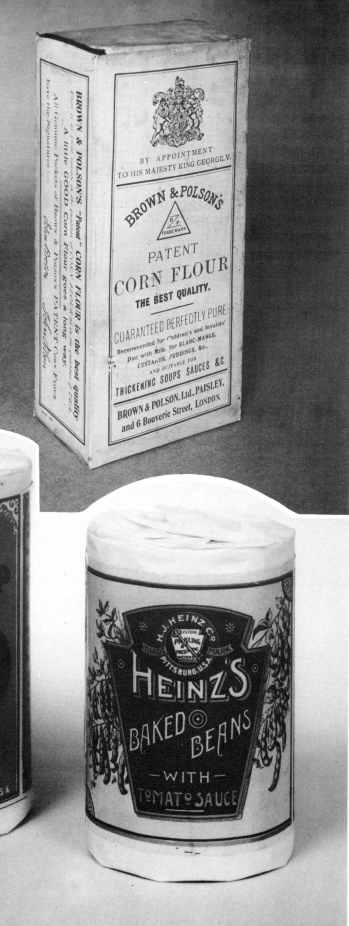

unashamedly as 'the best in the world', was sponsored by Miss Caroline Windsor, principal of the Croydon School of Cookery, who had used it for thirty years and still considered it to be the best. She was supported by the principals of cookery schools in Westminster, Bath, Eastbourne, Glasgow, South Kensington, Maidstone, the Isle of Wight, and the West of Scotland. G. Nelson, Dale & Co Ltd, manufacturers of gelatine, tablet and granulated jellies, pure mutton essence, granulated gravy, soups, custard powder and lemonade crystals among other goodies, published their recipe book under the name of 'Nelson's Comforts', complete with the coat of arms of the King of Spain, apparently a devoted user of their products.

B.t of

W. NAUNTON,
Fancy Bread & Biscuit Baker,
PASTRY COOK & CONFECTIONER.
Market Place. SWAFFHAM.
Wedding & other
Cakes, made to order.

FRENCH & BATH ROLLS MADE TO ORDER.

A. Burrell.

					£	s	d
April 9	Biscuits 1/ Baking 1					1	1
15	D.o 2					—	2
22	Buns 3 — D.o 1					—	4
	Biscuits 6					—	6
24	Cake 8.d Biscuits 4					1	0
	Baking 2½					—	2½
27	Bread D.o 10 D.o 5					1	3
	Biscuits 6					—	6
29	Bot. Cake 4/8					4	8
	Sponge 2/2.d					2	2
	Meal & Baking 8					1	3
	Sponge Cakes 6					—	6
30	Rolls 2/					2	—
May 10	Flour 4/2					4	2
12	Biscuits 1/					1	—
	Baking 2					—	2
	£					1	1	7½

Rec.d W. Naunton — 16 3½

June 26 1847 —

10 Billheads, Account Books and Manuscript Recipes

Old household bills, accounts and personal recipes are fascinating to read today, for they put flesh on the bare bones of kitchen life. They tell us about the kind of food eaten, the type of merchant from which it was purchased, current prices and quantities bought, and the general running of a well-ordered household.

Towards the end of the eighteenth century the owners of many businesses had developed their trade cards into a highly ornamental type of pictorial advertisement. These cards, which were about the size of a playing card, often bore elaborate engravings, as well as a description of the merchandise for sale. They were beautifully designed and printed, and were intended to attract the eye, and therefore business.

This type of card could also be used for rendering accounts, which were then written on the blank side. From these cards there developed the tradesman's bill, still headed by an elegant engraving, but on poorer paper with lower quality printing. Larger and more prosperous shopkeepers used pictorial representations of their businesses to head larger sheets of paper used as writing paper and also for bills. At the break-up of any old-established printer it may be possible to find some of the elegantly engraved blocks used for this purpose.

A simple bill can paint a vivid picture of a household and its tradesmen. An account rendered by R. Mountain, fishmonger and poulterer of Bury St Edmunds, Suffolk, to Mr Tanner at Christmas 1846 tells everything in a few words. Mr Mountain's bill features an elaborate engraving of a merman and mermaid supporting a shield with the motto of the Fishmongers' Company 'All Worship Be to God Alone'. Beneath this is a more prosaic picture of storage barrels and a collection of engravings of cods' heads, herrings, lobsters and assorted game. Mr Mountain, a licensed dealer in game, dealt wholesale and retail, with 'county orders punctually attended to'. He supplied 'Dried and Pickled Salmon, Haddocks, &c; Native & Other Oysters; Yarmouth Herrings; Sea Fish from the London Markets every Morning', and was also a dealer in Venison. Mr Tanner had been supplied with cod, oysters, lobster, turbot and salmon, and had a small bill outstanding from the previous year. He had also been credited with the supply of '8 Stone Paper', which presumably was used to wrap the fish, and which was allowed against his bill.

W. Naunton, fancy bread and biscuit baker, pastry cook and confectioner of Swaffham, Norfolk, rendered his bill to the late J. J. Clarke Esq on 26 June 1847. The items listed include flour, meal, biscuits, cakes, sponge cakes and rolls, and a baking charge is added to the bill.

Right R. C. Potter, linen and woollen draper, silk mercer and hatter, sold tobacco and snuff, as well as tea, groceries and Kent hops. His bill, dated 12 March 1846, for soap, moulds, candles, tea, mustard and gloves, shows a nice juxtaposition of engravings. On the left are two Chinamen surrounded by tea chests; on the right is a country funeral procession, complete with plumed horses.

From this bill it is possible to deduce the average stock of a large family business and the type of food purchased. Today, dried and pickled salmon, native oysters, Yarmouth herrings and venison are rarely available and certainly could not be supplied by a local fishmonger as a matter of course. Mr Mountain expected a daily delivery from London (some 70 miles distant) and would in his turn deliver quickly to county customers, but neither service could be expected today. He also took the burden of long credit, which appeared to be common practice, for many bills and account books indicate that provision merchants only expected annual settlement, and many customers took longer than twelve months. While some shops today still accept newspapers for wrapping purposes, they would certainly not allow for this in a customer's bill. Those who supplied wines and spirits were quicker to claim their money than the general stores. They gave only three months' credit, with 5 per cent. discount for monthly payment, and charged for all types of bottle.

Account books fall into two categories: those maintained by shopkeepers for individual customers, and those kept by the housekeeper or mistress of the house for recording her purchases. They range from simple notebooks to elaborately bound and printed books.

Christopher Corbold, who kept the account of Mr Mace from 1809–11, gave credit for almost two years on such items as loaves of sugar, Dutch cheese, starch, soap, oranges and lemons. He supplied large quantities of currants and far more spices than would be used by today's household, together with candles, brushes, corks, bay salt, and saltpetre for pickling.

Later account books show a wider range of goods supplied by grocers, and indicate changing tastes, decreasing self-sufficiency, and a lack of servants in middle-income households. A grocer in the mid 1860s was still supplying sugar, spices, saltpetre and vinegar for pickling, but he also sold the new baking powder, many varieties of pasta, and chicory to mix with coffee. He also supplied grapes and pippins alongside citrus fruit, for town families no longer maintained large kitchen gardens. Likewise they had neither the facilities nor servants to make their own cleaning materials, and the grocer supplied soft soap, curd soap, starch, soda, hearthstone and blacking, along with brooms and dustpans.

Careful householders liked to keep their own accounts, which reflect the life lived on large estates or in small individual houses. The Lister family of Shibden Hall in Yorkshire ate food grown and prepared on their estate, including beef, butter, cheese and cream, as well as bread, oatcakes and porridge made from their own home-grown and milled oats. Exceptional expenditure was carefully recorded:

9 October 1720 pd. Michael Vicers for Killing my Ox   1*s.* 6*d.*
11 October 1720 Received for an Ox hyde   1*s.* 2*d.*
15 October 1720 pd. for salt etc.   1*s.* 0*d.*

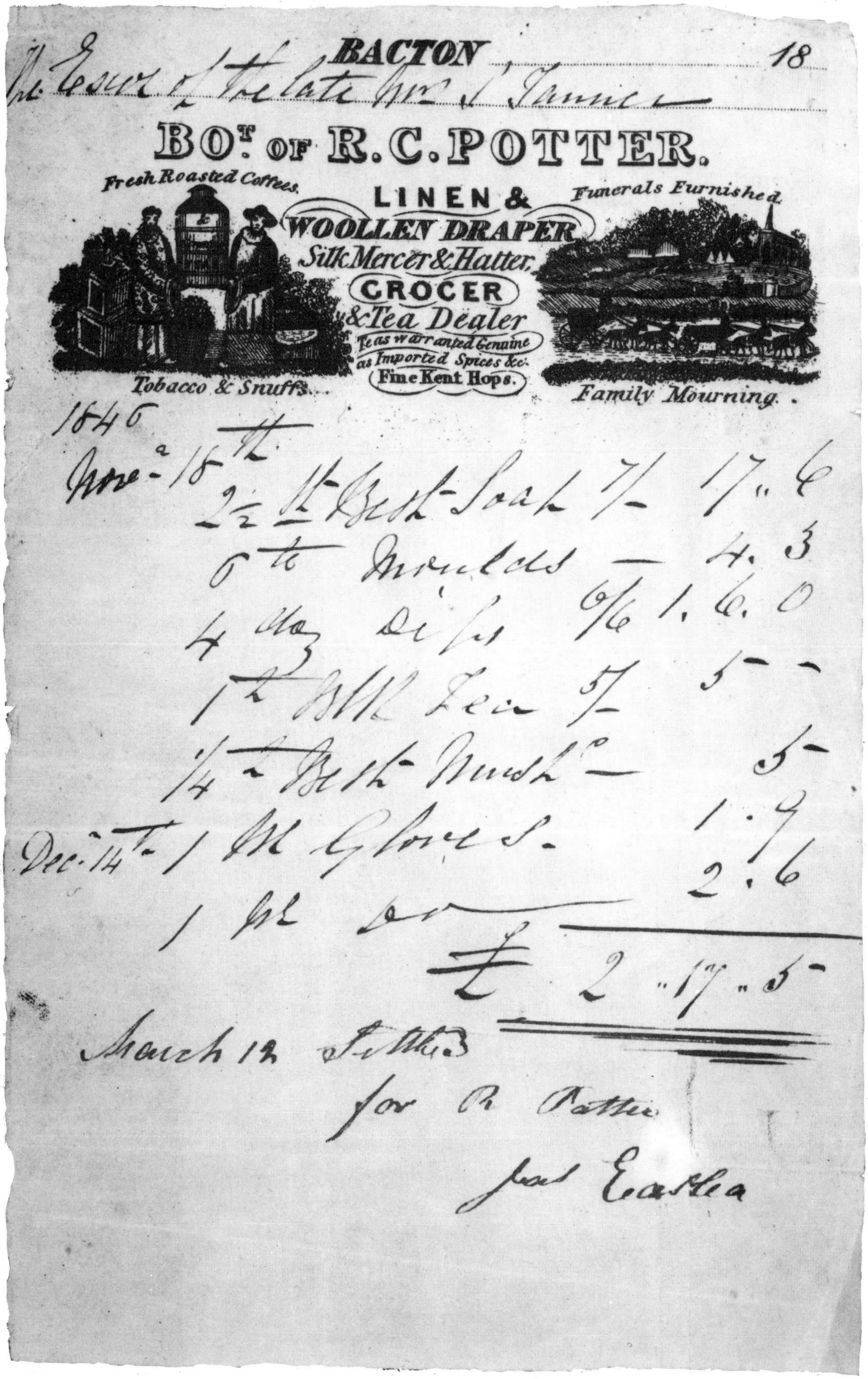

The Exors of the late Mr S Tanner

BOT. OF R. C. POTTER.

Fresh Roasted Coffees.

**LINEN &
WOOLLEN DRAPER**
Silk Mercer & Hatter,
GROCER
& Tea Dealer
Teas warranted Genuine
as Imported Spices &c.
Fine Kent Hops.

Funerals Furnished.

Tobacco & Snuffs.

Family Mourning.

1846

Nov.r 18th

2½ lb Best Soap	7/	17	6
6 lb Moulds	—	4	3
4 doz Dips	6/6	1. 6. 0
1 lb Bttr Tea	5/	5	—
¼ lb Bttr Brush	—	5	—
Dec.r 14th 1 Pr Gloves		1. 9
1 Pr do		2. 6
	£	2 " 17 " 5

March 12 Settled

for R Potter

Jas Easea

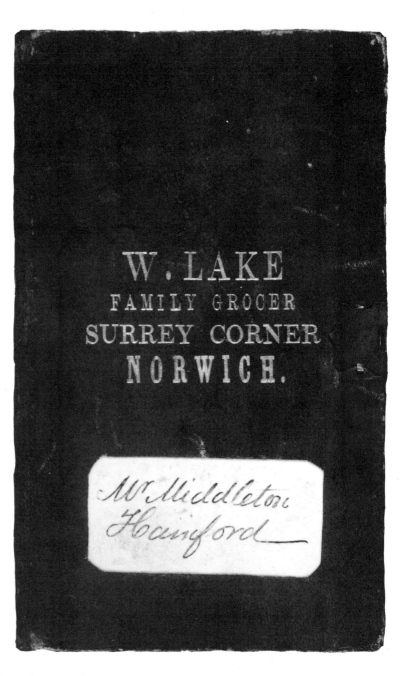

The salt was, of course, being used to preserve the meat for later use. In March 1722 James Lister celebrated the birth of his son Joseph with a party, buying wine, meat and bread, cheese from Robert Whiteheads, and the ingredients for a celebration drink—'a pint of Sack, Nutts, mace, Cinamon, Sugar'. In 1749 Uncle Lister's death entailed a funeral party, for which 4 lb funeral biscuits, half a gallon of red wine and half a gallon of white wine were purchased.

When the Rev. John Lister inherited the estate, he began to indulge in a more varied diet, buying many things which could not be grown or made on the estate. These included the following:

W. Lake, family grocer of Surrey Corner, Norwich, recorded his customers' purchases in a leather-bound account book. Settlement was usually made twice a year for a variety of items which include coffee, tea, chicory, lemons, raisins, cochineal, mace, sage, mustard, starch, vinegar, groats, sugar and soap.

5 doz. of oranges	4s. 2d.
Rice	3d.
Lemon, raisins & sugar	1s. 0d.
Black tea $\frac{1}{4}$ lb	1s. 10d.
Green tea $\frac{1}{4}$ lb	2s. 6d.

Asparagus	11d.
Coffee	1s. 6d.
Chocolate	1s. 1d.
A Cheshire Cheese 27$\frac{1}{2}$ lb	8s. 0d.
Scarboro Spa Water	8s.

In America there was even greater need for a self-supporting household and for the purchase of large quantities of food on rare shopping occasions. Rebecca Blanchard, wife of a Colonel who had commanded troops in the French and Indian Wars in 1755, entertained a great deal, and expected to salt down 100 lb of beef and 30 tongues at a time. In 1792 Abigail Adams, with a far smaller household (the Blanchards had fourteen children and many household slaves), ordered a barrel of brown sugar and 100 bushels of oats. Indeed, until the coming of the automobile, even town dwellers used to buy sugar, flour, apples and suchlike by the barrel to save trips to market. City people bought meat and fish from shops, but in the country it was customary to eat one's home-bred animals, and native fish and game caught in the appropriate season. Abigail Adams recorded having to leave her breakfast on the unexpected arrival of a drover, from whom she bought 'two spotted swine' to be killed for winter use.

At the end of the eighteenth and beginning of the nineteenth centuries rich Americans were able to import prestige food such as Gloucestershire and Cheshire cheeses, olive oil, claret, port and Madeira, and the cigars to accompany them. At the other extreme a farmer's wife would make do with honey, maple sugar or molasses instead of white sugar, and would feed the family on home-grown Indian meal and wild birds, animals or fish, and very occasionally a home-reared animal. During the course of a year she probably handled little more than $20 in cash, out of which she bought salt, tea and coffee, and small household items such as needles and knives.

In the nineteenth century specially printed housekeeping books were available for annual accounts with lists of items of likely expenditure. *The Economic Housekeeping Book* of 1862 listed, amongst other things, bacon, bread, butter, books, beer, cheese, candles, coal and wood, charitable donations, charwoman, eggs, earthenware, education, flour, fish, fruit, oatmeal and peas, rent, soda, starch and blue, travelling, taxes, wearing apparel and wages. Spaces were left for additional items. At various times in 1862 and 1863, one particular town housewife also listed expenditure on egg spoons, drawing-room clocks (£10), sunshade, Smith the porter, chair, soup, flowers, winter petticoat, poor woman, income tax (£1 16s. 6d.), Tunbridge ware and roses. She also included 2s. for Christmas pew opening and an annual donation of 1 guinea to the idiot asylum. Mad moments were indicated by the purchase of a barometer (3 guineas) and lovebirds (2 guineas); expenditure on a bird cage was not recorded until four weeks later. This particular housewife began to fail sadly, with the purchase of 'elastic for leg 4s. 8d', increasing sums spent on medicine and a weekly bill for the doctor. Her accounts ended abruptly in August 1863.

As shops became more prosperous and developed into department or chain stores, they issued catalogues for their regular customers, and sometimes for building up a new group of mail-order customers. These nineteenth-century lists reflect an increasing dependence on manufactured kitchen items, prepared foods, and household services. Department stores put out huge bound books offering every type of household requisite, garden furniture, stable fodder, groceries, cleaning materials and patent foods. In 1890 a London store like Harrods could offer such country delicacies as Devonshire and Dorset butter, eel pies, lunch cake and Yorkshire parkin, which would formerly have been prepared at home, alongside such sophistications as Lawn Tennis Cakes and Berlin Buns. Lists from caterers such as Buzzards reflect a trend for ostentatious balls and parties, which could no longer be catered for by the family chef or cook and servants.

Manufacturers, and some retailers, of early prepared foods issued simple broadsheets advertising their wares. These sheets were the forerunners of sponsored cookery booklets and leaflets which became a feature of the kitchen at the turn of the nineteenth century. Cooke & Co. of Hatton Garden, London, were advertising their curry pastes and sauces in 1830, and offering to supply merchants and captains at wholesale prices. They assured cooks that their products alone could produce the fashionable and popular curries as prepared in India, and they offered advice for boiling rice, and a variety of recipes. This broadsheet incorporated the familiar manufacturer's claim—'none are genuine unless signed by us'—later to be used as a guarantee of authenticity on powders, sauces and pickles of many types. This advertisement is also honest enough to admit that 'the Bengal Chattny Paste proved rather too piquante for the English bon vivantes, from the profusion of tears that were exhibited on some faces' at the Lord Mayor's Banquet in 1828.

The broadsheet, which often included somewhat extravagant claims, was also popular in America. In 1806 Isaac Thompson of New London, Connecticut, was advertising garden seeds. He maintained that he had 'correspondents' in various parts of the world, and that they had supplied him with the most extensive and best assortment of seeds, including an importation 'by the ship Bristol Packet, direct from London, warranted genuine, from the most eminent Seedsmen in England'.

Also in Connecticut, Nathaniel Townsend used his broadsheet as an advertisement in the *Norwich Packet* in 1793. He told his readers that he had hired a 'regular-bred Baker from Boston' and was prepared to send his 'Bread Carriage round from the upper part of the town, and through Chelsea, every day, except Sundays (designated by Slay Bells) about four-o'clock afternoon, with all those different kinds of bread which those that are pleased to patronise this undertaking shall require.' From his bakehouse 'in front of the Goal in Norwich' he proposed to sell, in large or small quantities, butter and groat biscuits, crackers, gingerbread, sugar and ginger cookies, rusks and buns.

Later lists from department and chain stores in the twentieth century indicated that the taste for biscuits, potted meats, pickles and sauces did not diminish, but there were no longer the cooks to prepare them, and branded goods were increasingly recognized.

It has been rightly said that there are more cooks than readers, and early cooks used few printed recipes. Recipes or 'rules', as they were often called, were passed from mother to daughter, and housewife to cook by word of mouth. It was pointless to write a recipe for a servant who could not read. The first printed English cookery book appeared in 1500, and another seventeen books were published in the next hundred years, although cookery manuscripts had been in existence in Britain since Alexander Neckham wrote his housekeeping book in 1157. From the middle of the seventeenth century the flow of cookery books

Mount Vernon

To make a great Cake

Take 40 eggs & divide the whites from the yolks & beat
them to a froth then work 4 pounds of butter to a cream &
put the whites of eggs to it a spoon full at a time till it
is well work'd then put 4 pounds of sugar finely powderd to
it in the same manner then put in the yolks of eggs & 5
pounds of flower & 5 pounds of fruit. 2 hours will bake it add
to it half an ounce of mace & nutmeg half a pint of wine & some
french brandy.

This was wrote by Martha Custis.
for her Grandmama

Recipe for a 'Great Cake', written out for Mrs Washington by her granddaughter, Martha Custis

increased, and English ones were used and reprinted by the American settlers until the first American cookbook by Amelia Simmons appeared in 1796.

Meanwhile, a few housewives felt it worthwhile recording their own favourite recipes and sometimes exchanged recipes with friends. These single recipes tend to appear on writing paper, sometimes with a printed address, although they have even been found on black-edged mourning paper used by families in times of grief. Such single sheets may be tucked into later printed cookery books or mixed in with a bundle of papers, bills, receipts and advertisements.

Those who kept personal recipe books sometimes used a small notebook or an almanac. These almanacs were printed with calendars of past and forthcoming events, and sometimes contained printed recipes, advertising matter or news of local events, but there were usually a few blank pages for the housewife's own notes. One English almanac of 1874, presented with 'M. E. Woole's best love', has hand-written recipes for curing tongues, stewed mushrooms, West India Pudding and Bishop's Cordial (a kind of blackcurrant gin). Notable events recorded in the printed pages included First Day Oysters—5 August; Dog Days End—11 August; Hare Hunting beginning and ending; University terms; a commemoration of the shooting of Admiral Byng 1757; expiry of fire insurance; Fire at Crystal Palace 1866; and a number of events in the Napoleonic and Crimea wars, which formed a curious background for homely recipes.

Those who took their housekeeping seriously kept larger bound books, in the form of commonplace books, recording not only recipes but also details of farm or cottage rents, pieces of poetry, cures for animals, and friends' addresses. These manuscripts give a far better picture of the diversity of housekeeping than any printed book of the same period.

Of course, many manuscript cookbooks consisted of recipes copied from printed books, but some had a more personal flavour. Martha Washington recorded her method of preserving cherries, and her favourite 'Great Cake' served at Mount Vernon on Christmas, Twelfth Night, and other festivals. She needed 40 eggs, which had to be divided into whites and yolks, and beaten to a froth, and 'frensh brandy'. The cake was matured by wrapping it in cheesecloth and soaking it in spirits for a month or more. This kind of extravagance is equalled in Oliver Hazara Perry's Recipe for Plumb Cake, which needed 'four pounds flour, four pounds currants, four pounds butter, four pounds sugar, four pounds citrion, one half an ounce mace, one half-pint brandy, forty eggs. Will make a devilish good wedding cake such as I had.' Thomas Jefferson's records at Monticello contain many interesting recipes, and he was particularly concerned with developing the use of sesame oil for salad dressing instead of the expensive imported European olive oil. The seed had originally been brought to Georgia by African negroes. Jefferson had decided to try and cultivate it for his own use, since a single bushel of seed would yield as much as 3 gallons of oil.

In 1836 Anne Lister of Shibden Hall, Halifax, built a new wing on to her house, including servants' quarters and a large kitchen. Here she recorded many new recipes and also forms of medicine, since the head of the household often had to prescribe for the family. Her 'Strengthning Jelly' included '4 quarts of water, two Vipers, One Quart of Snails wiped and brushed well, one pound of shavings of Hartshorn'.

A farmer commonly had to make up his own prescriptions for his animals. In 1823 Joseph Webb of Kent recorded his methods of dealing with scab in sheep, the murrain in a cow and a recipe for 'a nourishing drink for a cow'. Sometimes the prescriptions for items such as cough medicines were described as being suitable for the animals or the children. A 'Stomach Cordiall from Mrs Walter of Reading' needed '14 days shook up well in a stone bottle'. The kitchen also had recipes to follow 'to make good blacking', 'Tomata Sauce', 'Ginger Wine', 'Barm Yeast to Make the Best Bread and Cakes', 'To Pickle Mushrooms' 'To Improve Cider' and 'Sir Astley Cooper's Chilblain Salve'. They also had to be prepared to cure 'Bite of a Venemous Reptile', make Cold Punch in March with two gallons of best rum, and bottle gooseberries with a bladder over the bottle and an early sterilization method over the fire. The children were consoled with a fizzy drink of Persian sherbet, and a salad of apples, onions and hot peppers chopped finely in salt and vinegar. The household made its own vinegar and strong sauces, not to mention a lethal form of 'Beautiful Silver plating' from mercury stirred into nitric acid. Mr Webb was particularly happy to record the day he received his spaniel puppy from a neighbouring farmer.

A later commonplace book of 1847 is noteworthy for the record it gives of the gradual transition of country families to the towns. Mrs Elizabeth Garden kept a book which had originally belonged to her husband, when he was a pupil at Eton College in the 1830s, and the first pages are occupied by exercises in Greek and Latin and jokes about clergymen. When she married, she recorded the addresses of her favourite London and Paris shops, knitting patterns and hints on washing lace. She was fashionable in noting her favourite recipes for Tartare Sauce, Café Mousse, Minestrone and Sauce Bearnaise. Her servants, however, still came from the East Anglian countryside, where the family had originated. They were expected to roast swans, pickle hams, beef and pork, prepare sausages and pickled walnuts, grouse pie, harvest cakes, and homely dishes of stewed lentils with bacon or salt pork. They even needed to know how to keep mice out of the peas and how to prepare embrocation for rheumatism, although they lived in fashionable Victorian London.

Kitchens, Houses and Museums to Visit

Great Britain and Northern Ireland
Abbots Hall Museum of Rural Life, Stowmarket, Suffolk
The American Museum, Claverton Manor, Bath
Anne of Cleves House, Southover, Lewes, Sussex
Blakesley Hall, Birmingham
The Brighton Pavilion, Brighton, Sussex
Cambridge and County Folk Museum, Cambridge
The Castle Museum, York
Castle Ward, County Down, N. Ireland (National Trust)
Charlecote Park, Stratford-on-Avon, Warwickshire (National Trust)
Clandon Park, Surrey (National Trust)
Cotehele, Saltash, Cornwall (National Trust)
The Country Life Museum and Stedman Homestead, Aston Munslow, Shropshire
Easton Farm Park, Woodbridge, Suffolk
Filkins and Boughton Poggs Museum, Lechlade, Gloucestershire
The Geffrye Museum, Kingsland Road, London E2
Hardwick Hall, Derbyshire (National Trust)
Holkham Hall, Wells-next-the-Sea, Norfolk
Huntley House, Canongate, Edinburgh
Lacock Abbey, Wiltshire (National Trust)
Lanhydrock House, Cornwall (National Trust)
Longleat, Warminster, Wiltshire
Museum of English Rural Life, Reading, Berkshire
The Museum of Staffordshire Life, Shugborough, Great Haywood, Staffordshire
The Mustard Shop, Bridewell Alley, Norwich
North Cornwall Museum and Gallery, Camelford, Cornwall
Ordsall Hall Museum and Peel Park, Salford, Lancashire
Ryedale Folk Museum, Hutton-le-Hole, York
Saltram House, Plympton, Plymouth, Devon (National Trust)
The Science Museum, South Kensington, London SW7
Shibden Hall, Halifax, Yorkshire
Stanford Hall, Lutterworth, Leicestershire
Strangers' Hall Museum, Charing Cross, Norwich
Sulgrave Manor, Banbury, Oxfordshire
Wallington, Cambo, Northumberland (National Trust)
Washington Old Hall, Tyne and Wear (National Trust)
The Welsh Folk Museum, St Fagans, Cardiff, Glamorganshire
The William Cookworthy Museum, Kingsbridge, Devon

United States of America
Colonial Williamsburg, Virginia
Greenfield Village & Henry Ford Museum, Dearborn, Michigan
Joshua Hempsted House, New London, Connecticut
Mount Vernon, Virginia
Old Salem Inc., Winston-Salem, North Carolina
Old Sturbridge Village, Sturbridge, Massachusetts
Pennsylvania Farm Museum of Landis Valley, Lancaster, Pennsylvania
Van Cortlandt Manor, Croton-on-Hudson, New York

Sources of Illustrations

references to position on page are
in *italic*
references to colour plates are in
heavy type

Index